BEYOND BELIEF

The Miracle of a Broadland Business

Anne Murrin

ISBN: 978-1-912420-16-2

Printed and bound in the UK by Witley Press Ltd
www.witleypress.co.uk

Also available on Amazon as an e-book

I am hoping this book will give courage to those who are timid, comfort to those who feel oppressed, hope for those who are despairing, confidence to those who are attempting to fulfil dreams, faith to those who are wavering, and a Light for those having to take pathways into the unknown.

The Author

DEDICATION

This book is dedicated to Philip Howard, my fellow Samaritan and mentor, who encouraged me on the path to education which opened so many doors without which the main part of this story may never have occurred. He also nagged me on the path to writing. Sadly, he died in January 2017 and was never to see the book published.

I would also like to dedicate the book to my seven grandchildren; Tom, Izzy, Alice, Livy, Lucy, Rowan and Erin for whom it may act as an inspiration and encouragement.

CONTENTS

ENDORSEMENTS

"The twists and turns of everyday life can knock our confidence, making us question our worth to ourselves, to others and to God - but this inspiring book reassures us that it's at times when we feel most vulnerable and inadequate that we discover the true depth and strength of God's love. Anne Murrin writes movingly about the many challenges she's faced on her life's journey, through which she's gradually learned that trust in the eternal love of God is the key to unlocking ability and potential. This book is a generous sharing of trial and triumph, and powerful lessons learned along the way."

Pam Rhodes, *BBC Television's SONGS OF PRAISE*

"Through her book, Beyond Belief, Anne Murrin describes the way in which she learned to deal with disability and all the things life threw at her, by staying positive and maintaining her sense of self belief and humour. As a wheelchair user myself, I can relate to many of the things Anne describes; from the insensitivity of others, to the general difficulty of being in a wheelchair. I hope disabled people reading the book understand that they aren't alone with the issues they face and that able-bodied people may gain some more sensitivity to those issues and realise that a wheelchair shouldn't mean exclusion. As humans, we are all different, and those differences should be embraced and not avoided."

Jordanne Whiley MBE, *Paralympian*

"What a proof that faith in God can help in all circumstances. Anne's witness is full of courage, joy and hope."

David Payne, *Director of Catholic Faith Exploration (CaFE)*

"Anne's way of being, her acceptance of the challenges and experiences which have been given to her, makes her book an example to others of the resilience and courage that can be gained from the dross that life can throw at us. We need to keep walking with those 'footprints' beside us."

June Taylor, Reg. *Member of the British Association for Counselling and Psychotherapy*

"I really enjoyed reading the extracts Anne sent me from her book. Her story is told with a warmth which is a delight. The memory of Anne that I will always have is of me going out to her office to discuss the sale of her business, expecting to be met, as previously, by a seemingly old Lady in a wheelchair, and instead being met by someone apparently 10 years younger with enormous energy. The sheer delight on my face as I realised this was Anne, miraculously improved, and most of all the look on Anne's face as she watched my reaction. It still warms my heart to remember that moment."

Philip Needham, BA (Hons) FCA, *Director, Hornbeam Accountancy Services*

"This book demonstrates that there is a tremendous power within each of us that sometimes needs unlocking. Occasionally it takes a crisis to achieve this. Anne's book shows how, by plumbing the depths, we can begin to recognise we are not alone in our endeavours, and amazing things can happen, even in our ordinary everyday lives. We simply have to open our eyes and trust in that Power."

Dr John Clements, *Pastor of the Old Meeting House, Congregational Church, Norwich. Author of 'How to GetWhat Money Can't Buy'*

FOREWORD

 Anne Murrin has produced an autobiographical study of compelling interest. Her life has been anything but easy and she has known the pain of divorce, the challenges of single parenthood, the torment of psychological breakdown and, increasingly, the physical ordeal of a condition of the spine which has led to crippling disability and wheel-chair occupancy.

In no way, however, is the book a mournful experience for the reader. On the contrary, it tells the remarkable story of the motivational energy which led to the creation of a unique management and lettings business and of the experiences of a woman in a leadership role at a time when few women occupied such positions.

The book is inspirational for it demonstrates that setbacks and much suffering can be the context for achievement and spiritual development of a high order. Anne Murrin has all her life been on the road to her spiritual home and her story tells of the fidelity of a God whose guiding hand has often led her to take some unexpected turnings.

This is a book which offers much solace to the despairing and immense encouragement to those who refuse to relinquish hope even in the darkest hour. It is also beautifully written.

Brian Thorne

Emeritus Professor of Counselling, University of East Anglia.
Co-founder of the Norwich Centre for personal, professional and
spiritual development.
Lay Canon, Norwich Cathedral

ACKNOWLEDGEMENTS

My deepest gratitude goes to Dr John Clements for his patience and guidance without whose help this book might never have reached publication. I am also very thankful to Lidia Suszycka for her great artistic talent and inspired interpretation for the cover design for this multi-faceted story, and to Sue Garner, Charles Carver and Nick Greef for their checking and proof reading.

I have mentioned many people by name in this book who also deserve thanks, including those alluded to (who will hopefully recognise themselves on reading the story). Without their influences in my life, intended or otherwise, there might not have been a story worth telling. Not to be forgotten also are the autobiographical books written by personalities known to me. Their autobiographical soul-barings have also been a great inspiration and encouragement, particularly at times when I was wilting at the thought of such personal self-exposition.

Deserving thanks also are my parents for giving me such a good grounding, my siblings for honing my edges, and not forgetting my children, and particularly my grandchildren, for whom the kernel of this story was originally intended.

The biggest gratitude of all must go to God's Spirit within who guided my hand at every turn, giving me the courage to bare my soul, thus expanding the story to its final outcome.

--ooOoo—

PREFACE

How often have you been in the depths of despair? Or hit a brick wall when attempting a project? Or even just wondered what your next move should be? Have you taken risks and then feared for the folly of the undertaking? Have you undertaken anything challenging at all?

A sense of achievement can be hugely uplifting. This book is the true story of someone who found herself thrown into most of these situations and her attempts at scrambling out, and it records some of the adventures along the way.

The writing began as an enterprise to record one of the achievements - the history of the business I set up in the late nineteen-eighties as a means of supporting my young family after a physically abusive marriage. My original purpose in highlighting this piece of history was originally for the benefit of my grandchildren, and maybe future generations, by way of inspiration where talents and confidence might need to be encouraged.

The business was unique in that it was the first of its kind in its 'modus operandi', in Norfolk at least, and it was begun at a time when women mostly occupied the more menial employed positions in the working world. As such, there is an element of social history attached to the story, too.

It became apparent, as pen took to paper (or, more truthfully, fingers to keyboard), that there was a need to explain the reasons behind why the business had to be set up. Also, as the business developed, so also did a spinal problem that brought me close to total incapacity, and this inevitably became intertwined in the story. As memories came flooding back, I became even more aware that the events regarding the establishment and running of the business, and the events surrounding my own physical (and mental) circumstances, have at times, been quite beyond belief. Inevitably there was a Power at work that was beyond my own strength, and that kept me going against the odds, and in Whose control I began to trust implicitly.

As a Charismatic Christian attending various conferences and meetings, I began to realise that there was a huge amount of testimony involved in this story, very similar to what was being recounted by others at these events. Not only that, but at each attendance at these meetings, the promptings became stronger and stronger that I should be doing something comparable in witnessing to God's involvement in my life. Not being good at speaking in public, maybe writing was how it should be accomplished. The business, therefore, seemed to become a vehicle through which to demonstrate how God works in our daily lives. As such, this story could have a triple purpose, history, witness and inspiration.

It took some three years of these promptings before I finally succumbed and plucked up the courage to respond with a 'Yes!' (forever the procrastinator!). The writing became a little more expansive as I began converting my record into a manuscript more suitable for general publication.

I have attempted to write the story as neutrally as possible so that it would be acceptable to a wider audience, some of whom, on reading the account, might be inspired to a deeper belief without being put off by too much religiosity. However, the Hand guiding my hand seemed to have had other ideas. I had to 'Let go, let God'. I hope the final style adopted does not put off those of lesser or no faith. After all, I must trust He knows what He is doing!

There are reflections at the end of each chapter to provoke deeper thought for those who wish, and questions to encourage discussion where the book might be used in groups. Or it can simply be read as a story ignoring the tailpieces.

--ooOoo--

Chapter 1

IN THE BEGINNING

PRELUDE

Way Ahead

In the late 1960s I read George Orwell's novel '1984' – a rather awesome prediction of how life on this earth could become. The year seemed eons ahead. Little did I realise at the time the phenomenal changes that were to occur to a rather naïve and very timid product of the Baby Boom years – myself. The year 1984 became a major catalyst for my transformation but thankfully not for the rest of the world as Orwell had predicted.

Heron was the enterprise that was eventually to plant me firmly on my feet once and for all, but how it came to conception was equally important. It was a concept that took some years in its realisation. It was born out of a need. Once born, and initially nameless, it had to be pushed and shoved and nagged into full existence. As I say, it all started in 1984 – well, there was something of a lead-up in the preceding years, in the preceding five years in particular - and it all began with a Samaritan, two, or even three in fact …

There were other significant occurrences, particularly a spiritual transformation that occurred many years earlier that was to underpin all that went on after 1984, but it was this particular year that triggered my growth in stature, self-esteem and above all, developed my trusting faith.

The Need

In 1979 I became the separated, and subsequently divorced, mother of three young children aged between three and eight. I had no income and no maintenance for the children or myself. We did have a roof over our heads of which I owned a part, thanks to some mysterious manipulation by my divorce solicitor. He had somehow managed to land me with half a small bungalow and a mortgage for the other half which was both a blessing and a burden.

How was I to pay our way forward and keep body and soul together, and those of three children? My earning capacity was hampered by three things: the need to care for these three young children traumatised by the events that made the divorce essential; my own situation of being in the early stages of recovery from a state of complete nervous exhaustion; and the fact that the only qualifications I had were of a secretarial nature. Wages in Norfolk were such that any income I could derive from employment with these latter qualifications would be insufficient for me to be able to crawl out of the State benefit trap.

Career Cares

The idea of becoming a mere secretary was the last thing that had been on my career list as a teenager. I was torn between so many options when I left school; hospital almoner (nowadays referred to as a hospital social worker), occupational therapist, radiographer, vet - I wanted to do something 'special' but just could not decide what. I thought about university but didn't think I had the confidence to go. Besides, my Father was reluctant to pay any further educational costs as he felt he had done his bit by paying for private education to the age of 16 for me and my siblings. No mean feat when there were six of us.

Also, I was a female, and in my Father's eyes a woman's principal task in life was to get married and manage a family. It was the early '60s and times were changing rather faster than my Father could keep up with. This did not help my dilemma about how I was to gainfully occupy myself in the meantime until a suitable suitor became available to enable me to become the manager of this desired family. My choice of career, and the desire for it to be something rather special, became one of the most troublesome bothers of my mid-teen years.

To give me more time to think, my Father suggested doing a secretarial course because he claimed it would be "always useful". The idea of putting such qualifications into practice did not appeal but I liked the idea of the 'extra time to think'. So I was duly enrolled and set off for the Pitman College in Pelham Street, Nottingham, to begin my education into the lower echelons of the world of commerce.

Going Slow

Shorthand appealed as I found the Pitman version quite artistic. However, I quickly learned this was not the point and my beautiful chirography was wasted once I found I had to mount up my speed to 100 wpm or more. The best I achieved was around 60 wpm.

Then there was the typing. This turned out, for me, to be more like a physical exercise class. We had to learn to type in time to the tune of "William Tell" and at the end of each line we had to throw the carriage back to start a new line without losing speed. At the completion of these exercises my fingers were tripping over each other so that the result frequently resembled a dyslexic's dither. Being of a somewhat pedantic nature, my speeds for both shorthand and typing were to remain painfully slow – a steamroller could have

3

passed across a keyboard or page faster than my fingers would allow if I was to get the words down correctly.

I was not expecting to do well in my exams at the end of the year but I can't recall being too bothered about it. I had had a good year socially after years of being incarcerated in a rural convent boarding school, and I had met some interesting girls - some already in employment. These employees had been given time out to study to advance themselves within their companies, their courses mostly paid for by their employers. Some students were achieving typing speeds of up to 60 words per minute – my best was 32 wpm. I was never actually to find out how I compared under the duress of an exam, for the day before the first of my secretarial exams I received a letter in the post that would eventually change the course of my life.

LIFE CHANGING

Shockwaves

I had been attending the Hospital routinely following a chest infection. Some months earlier, after experiencing what appeared to be a 'flu-type virus, our GP had suggested I attend one of the mass x-ray clinics prevalent in the '60s set up to try and eradicate tuberculosis from the population. The first x-ray showed a small shadow on my upper left lung. This, I was told, could be an old scar where the body had naturally overcome the disease – nevertheless, they wished to keep it under observation.

There followed six months of repeated x-rays, sputum tests, and clinical examinations – each time the result was negative. Friends and relatives all said I looked too well to have anything wrong with me. Then one day, following such a check-up, I received a letter from the hospital asking me to attend a Consultant's appointment accompanied by a parent or guardian. I had no inkling even then that anything might be amiss.

What the Consultant told us sent both my Mother and me into a state of shock. The TB had become active. I was stunned. I tried to mitigate the shock with thoughts of being sent to Switzerland for the pure mountain air that was supposed to be good for such a disease.

Switzerland

I had spent the previous Christmas in Arosa with my Belgian Uncle Robert and his family as a special treat, and to learn to ski, and had found it beautiful. Robert was my Mother's eldest brother. A great Aunt came with us too. She brought the turkey with her which we hung outside the window of the chalet to keep it chilled. An enduring memory of this special holiday was walking to Midnight Mass on Christmas Eve. Various church bells were ringing across the frozen lake from the town below as we walked through the night, with only moon and stars reflecting on the snow, and the twinkling lights from the town in the valley. We had torches for additional guidance as we tramped through the forest to the small chapel, tucked away deep in the woods. It was illuminated only by candles.

Frustration

I was not to return to this beautiful country - no such luck. Nor was I to be sent to a sanatorium. I was told that, as the disease had been caught in its very early stages, it would be more sensible for me to be treated at home, in isolation, rather than being sent to a TB hospital where my parents' visits would put them at greater risk of bringing the disease home to my five younger siblings - the youngest being merely two years of age at the time.

Complete bed-rest with the least movement possible was prescribed. I was not allowed to knit or sew, draw or paint – just watch TV and

5

read, for six whole months, in isolation, at home. For someone who was very active and loved dancing, competitive sport, and cycling out to open country from the suburbia in which we lived on the outskirts of Nottingham, this treatment seemed like torture at its most extreme.

I didn't even feel ill. Normal life carried on outside the confines of my bedroom to torment me even further - not just within the home, for my bedroom overlooked the road also - and I was allowed no visitors. There were times when I ranted and raged (which probably did me more harm than if I had taken up knitting or sewing!) I was a cradle Catholic and the God whom I had been brought up to believe in frequently bore the brunt of my anger, and so did my undeserving parents.

My Parents

My parents did their best. In retrospect, I could have used the time to read the many books, classic and otherwise, that I wish I had the time for nowadays. I had no one to guide me with suggestions. My Father was non-academic, always joking that, in order to become top of the class when at school, one would have had to turn the class upside down. He hadn't even needed to find himself a career path as this was settled for him from birth – there was a family business with management positions, and subsequently directorships, awaiting him and his two brothers.

My Mother was Belgian and had her education interrupted by the War. Her family lived on the Belgian coast in a town now known as De Panne where my Grandparents ran a Pharmacy. She was 18 when she and her siblings were evacuated and sent to stay with their Aunts in Brussels – these were five spinster sisters who lived together. Their spinsterhood derived from the shortage of available men of marriageable age as a result of the First World War casualties. As the eldest girl, my Mother was expected to take care of her younger siblings during their evacuation, while her parents tried to keep the Pharmacy going in the war zone.

The building in which my Grandparents lived, which also housed the Pharmacy, sported three flats above which were normally let out to holidaymakers. During the War the flats were offered as accommodation for British Army personnel. My Father was posted to Dunkirk, just across the border, and happened to be one of the lucky soldiers to be billeted at my Grandparents' home. On a visit home one weekend, my Mother found the place full of British soldiers and was invited to join them at a dance in the town.

So began the romance of my parents, and my Mother's move straight from sibling-minding into marriage, and then minding her own children, all in fairly quick succession. I was born eleven months following their wedding, with my sister Liz arriving 14 months later. By the end of nine years there were five of us in total, followed by another brother, Paul, born eight years later - sixteen years is the gap between his age and mine. So my poor Mother hardly had time to think for herself, let alone familiarise herself with British culture. For me, the War had been a lucky experience – we lost no members of the family as a result and, without the war, my parents would not have met. The principal worrying time for the family was when my Belgian Grandfather was imprisoned by the Germans for listening to the BBC.

School Days

The school I was sent to for secondary education was a small convent boarding school near Tamworth in Staffordshire. It was a lovely school with its own farm and run by quite a liberal order of nuns, the Sisters of St Joseph of Cluny. I remember my Father being most put out because, in the autumn term, instead of the usual games periods, we were sent potato picking. He felt that, as he was paying for our schooling, it was not right that we were being used as free labour. At the end of the day I saw it as good exercise, out in the fresh air, which is where we would have been anyway had we been doing sport, and it was only for half a term - but I could see my Father's point.

We numbered 105 pupils from the ages of 5-18. My largest class one year had twelve pupils – most years we were six, and one year only three, so it was not difficult to become top of the class, or to be chosen as Head Girl. The curriculum was also very narrow, with only eight subjects to choose from for 'O' levels. All in all, my education and experience of life (my Father being in a family business, and my parents having little time to socialise either) was very narrow. I suppose I became quite frustrated as a teenager as a result.

Transformation

Being incarcerated as I was by my illness, with little of interest to occupy my time, only added to this frustration. I had to settle with my own thoughts for company and what I could glean from the television, but with no chance to take part in discussions or debates.

One day, in a complete fit of pique which triggered in me some deep thinking, I was coming to the conclusion that there was the possibility that this God that I was supposed to believe in did not actually exist. How could a God allow such a cruel thing to happen to someone so young, who had such energy, and who had only just begun to savour the Big Wide World after years in the confines of a convent boarding school? And this was the Sixties!

No, this God, if he did exist, had let me down big time. He was supposed to be benevolent. These things were not compatible. After all, God seemed to be in my Mother's thinking only. My Father and his family, with whom we mostly socialised, were non-practising Anglicans. The exception was my Grandmother who attended her

8

church quite regularly. Dad supported my Mother in bringing us up in the Faith as he had promised at marriage. But whatever his thoughts might have been, he gave no visible signs of belief himself. And of course, the Catholic schools I had been sent to, by their very nature, were bound to promote belief. I finally decided I definitely could no longer believe in this God, he did not exist.....

Before the thought had taken a complete grip on my mind I had the most incredible experience. God's most holy presence completely engulfed me. It filled my being with such joy and feeling of closeness to Him – I was enraptured. It was a very real experience of His Mystical Being. I was on 'Cloud Nine'. This new, deep relationship with this Supreme Being was bliss beyond any earthly description. From that day on I could never again doubt His existence.

Was this what we now refer to as 'Baptism in the Holy Spirit'? It was 1964. In my naïve state of faith as it was then, my knowledge was principally of God the Father and I was not fully familiar with the workings of the Holy Spirit in our lives at that time. No one was praying over me (though I learnt after my recovery that many had been praying for me – particularly the nuns at my old School from where, it transpired, I had contracted the disease), and I was completely alone when the experience took place.

This state of euphoria remained for many years after. I wondered whether perhaps God was calling me to become a nun, but on consideration I realised my spirit and physicality were far too restless to be constrained by convent life. However, after the experience, I did find material things no longer of much consequence. When I had recovered from the TB my parents wanted to take me out for a special dinner as a treat – I told them that, although I was grateful for the offer, they would be wasting their money (and this despite my love of food!). I seemed to be spiritually nourished and this was enough

9

to keep me more than happy. ("God alone is enough" – St Teresa of Avila).

Another amazing, one could say miraculous, experience was yet to follow …

Evangelisation

I had only one visitor during this time, our Parish Priest who happened also to be the Diocesan Financial Administrator. We had been attending another local parish and I had rather hoped that one of the younger curates would be my visitor. Living in the suburbs of Nottingham we had a choice each Sunday of attending a variety of Masses, timed almost 15 minutes apart, at four different churches, and all within a two-mile radius. Our actual parish was our least attended as it was in a slum area, so it was a bit of a disappointment when this somewhat elderly priest, a Canon to boot, was to become my only visitor for the next six months.

By coincidence, his ministry in a previous parish had included a TB sanatorium. He refused to take the advised precautions of remaining at the foot of the bed, visiting me regularly with Holy Communion and remaining afterwards for a chat. He quickly learnt of my penchant for anything to do with words and bought me my first Thesaurus and a dictionary, and word puzzles to keep me occupied. He never discussed religious matters as I often wished he would, but I was too naïve on the subject, and too shy to ask.

Selflessness witnessed in action is a wonderful evangeliser. This Parish Priest continued to visit even when I was convalescing and easing back into normal life. My Father, who did not share my Mother's and her offspring's Catholic faith, had, since the Canon's visits, begun to show an interest in coming to belief. Beside me still being on his visiting list, there materialised two further reasons for this dear Canon to continue his visits to our household; the

10

evangelisation of my Father, and the additional enticement of my Mother's 'spag-bol' (spaghetti Bolognese) for which he had a penchant - as did my Father, and it was a great ruse to get them talking.

Holy Smoke!

On one of these visits during my convalescence, Fr Allen came with a special request. Would I be prepared to help temporarily with the Bishop's secretarial work until they could find a replacement, as the Bishop's secretary had given her notice? I was quite dumbstruck. I said I would have to think about it as I was already occupied part-time back at college, taking a refresher course to complete my secretarial qualifications.

I had never wanted to be a mere secretary but could think of no more fulfilling career than being personal secretary to a Bishop, especially in my current state with this new-found relationship with God. I had wanted to do something 'special' as a career. Surely this was the 'something special' I had yearned for, albeit in a secretarial guise! However, the position being offered was only as a stop-gap.

When the Canon returned for my reply I told him that I would love to help so long as it could be considered a permanent position - and I would even be prepared to give up my exams. My audacity was soon to be deflated – I was told the Bishop was looking ideally for someone more mature (I was by then not quite 19). Despite this, he offered to discuss my proposal with the Bishop.

For nearly five years, until marriage moved me away to Cardiff, I had the most rewarding, fulfilling and unbelievable career – an answer to prayer that could not have been dreamed of. This would never have come about but for the very negative experience of my illness. God surely works in mysterious ways and quite frequently with a sense of humour! The Bishop's work was not quite full-time so I was still able

11

to complete the college work on a part-time basis and take my exams. Thereafter, in order to make it a full-time job, any balance of time would be spent in the Diocesan Financial Office helping our Canon with the accounts.

The Moral

There were two morals I learnt from this experience: to have patience in waiting for answers to prayer because with God all time is present - time being a man-made phenomenon. More importantly, even in one's darkest moments, never doubt God's plan for you.

Ultimately, one must learn to trust which can be incredibly hard. Unless one hits rock bottom, only then are there no options left but to trust. After that, everything becomes a bonus, a gift from God. I remember making a vow to myself during my illness that when I recovered I would embrace life with complete zest, occupying each day as fully as my energy would allow, doing everything possible that was within my capabilities within this wonderful creation.

I began by re-engaging with my love of tennis, though this sport was becoming increasingly difficult with the recurrence of spinal problems that had first manifest at age fifteen. Cycling seemed easier, and my love of dancing was rekindled when our dancing teacher asked my friend and I to assist her at a local public school to help teach the sixth form boys ballroom and Latin-American dancing.

With this new-found trust in the Lord, the boundaries of capability can become amazingly stretched, as I was eventually to find out.

VOCATION

Work Experience

My miserably slow shorthand and typing speeds, which just scraped me through the exams, I need not have worried about – not that it was ever a particular concern of mine as I had never actually intended to become a secretary anyway. The Bishop was so ponderous in his dictation that I had no problem taking down what he said as he spoke – I could, and sometimes did, write it down in longhand. With one exception; every so often he would insert a Latin phrase without warning. Somehow I would hear this as a continuation of the English dictation and what I typed often had an interpretation rather variant to the Latin version he intended.

I had learnt Latin at school but, being the very small school it was, we could only take Latin if we achieved a certain mark in our French exams. French was my Mother's native language so I was reasonably good at it. After two years, the other pupils had gradually dropped away because of poor marks and I ended up being the only one left in the Latin class. "You don't need Latin for most careers nowadays" I was told – a euphemism for saying "There is no point in teaching one pupil", and I had to drop the subject.

How were these teaching nuns to know that I would end up in the one job where a greater knowledge of Latin would have been such a tremendous asset? The career options they steered us towards were teaching, nursing and housewifery. What teaching talents I may have had, I wished to reserve for my own children, assuming I would be blessed with some. I could not stand the sight of blood, so nursing was out of the question. I needed a fulfilling stopgap before opting for the third option. This I had now found, or rather it had fortuitously found me.

On reflection, God's plan for me was quite remarkable. If I had known earlier how to trust I could have spared myself some considerable teenage angst, both concerning my inability to choose a career, and regarding the frustrations of my illness.

Job Description

Bishop's House was situated in The Park, an upmarket housing area close to the centre of Nottingham. The Bishop had a priest Assistant who worked in the adjoining office, and the housekeeping was undertaken by three live-in nuns who, each morning, brought me tea on a tray. This was accompanied by biscuits and sometimes cake if they had been baking, and this was repeated in the afternoon - if I was still around and had not moved on to the accounts office. This was a short walk away, next door to the Cathedral in the centre of Nottingham.

My tasks as the Bishop's Office Secretary were: to take dictation and type up transcripts of books and Pastoral letters; correspondence with parish priests and seminarians - frequently spattered with the aforementioned Latin quotes without warning. The nuns' short-sightedness regarding teaching me Latin had the effect at times, with my English interpretation, of causing quite some hilarity in the office at Bishop's House! Then there were letters to the occasional famous personage (and the not-so-famous complainants), and numerous odd jobs of a PA nature. As this was the time of Vatican II, there was, of course, correspondence directly with the Pope, too.

Among some of the more interesting tasks I encountered was typing up a detailed diary after the Bishop's annual salmon fishing holidays in Ireland. I could almost take up salmon fishing myself with the knowledge I gained from these diaries! One of the precursor events to these holidays, for me, would be the making up of the colourful flies for attaching to the end of the line used to attract the fish. At the end of a day's work, on returning home to the family, we often shared a recounting of our day's activities. The family found it highly amusing when, one day, I announced that part of my day had involved "doing the Bishop's flies". Most of what I did, of course, was highly confidential.

The Husband-to-be

One of the activities I had indulged in during my illness was to learn German from the television. Fortunately, in the '60s, there was a quantity of educational programmes one could follow, including Open University courses. The only times I had been abroad prior to Switzerland was to Belgium to visit the relatives, and they all spoke English as well as French so no problem with feeling 'at home' with the languages there. The Swiss town of Arosa was in one of the German-speaking cantons of Switzerland and I had found myself most frustrated that I could not understand a word of what went on whilst I was there. My incarceration seemed an opportune time to remedy this situation.

It became quite difficult to continue learning from the TV after my recovery with so many other distractions around, so I set off to enrol for an evening class. Unfortunately, the class was full. When my Father heard this, he told me he was sending a couple of his sales team to a class to learn Beginners' German for Business. My Father suggested that this was unlikely to be very different from learning ordinary everyday German, certainly in the first year, so I duly enrolled.

Because of drop-outs in the second year, reducing the numbers in both German classes, the classes were combined. It was in the remnants of the other class that I found the man I was eventually to marry, despite having been the only female in the previous year's 'Business' class. We seemed to have a lot of similar interests and we

15

would chat in the coffee breaks. This progressed into doing our homework together. The rest is history. I suppose I saw in him someone who was very knowledgeable, self-made (he had a good managerial post in a joinery manufacturing company) and confident. We seemed very compatible. He was very different to my Father.

~

REFLECTION:

TOUCHED BY GOD

Many people have asked me over time "Why have I not had a direct experience of the Holy Spirit?" It is a question that is not easy to answer. I have known many good and prayerful people who have prayed for, and received prayer for, a special infilling of the Holy Spirit and nothing spectacular has happened. I also know of one lady who had not even been baptised but who came along to a 'Life in the Spirit' course simply to accompany her husband. When she was offered prayer for an encounter with the Spirit, she firstly declined, then later changed her mind. As she was receiving prayer she experienced the most amazing infilling of the Holy Spirit and her life changed completely. She became a baptised Christian and now spends much of her time doing wonderful work in the name of Jesus.

Some people are envious of such experiences. However, there are some facts to bear in mind: Firstly, it does not make those who have not received such a special blessing any less valued in the sight of God. Granted they might have to work harder to keep up the strength of their faith, but that is a virtue itself. Secondly, it is possible that those who have received such spiritual encounters are being prepared for some tough challenges ahead which the Spirit in their lives will fortify. Thirdly, they are not necessarily 'good' people who experience such blessings. Witness some of the saints who led less than exemplary lives before their conversions. St Paul, in particular, before his conversion, was actually persecuting Christians. And St Peter, chosen by Jesus to be head of His Church on earth, who betrayed Him (Luke 22:61-62), argued with Him and even, at times, lacked faith, despite having such first-hand experience of God's Son, and being directly imbibed with His teaching. Both experienced persecution during their ministry and both their lives ended in martyrdom.

We are all equal in the sight of God whether we have received a special touch or experience, or not. We can achieve a very close encounter with Him through persistent prayer. God's ways are indeed mysterious and we must remember that we are made by Him with differing talents and strengths and He has a plan for each of us accordingly (Jeremiah 29:11-13) – we have only to trust.

THOUGHTS FOR DISCUSSION

1. Are you convinced that God looks on you with caring and loving eyes as He does the rest of His created beings?

2. How convinced are you that God has a plan for you?

3. How does it make you feel to think that some of the greatest personages in the Church's history had been great sinners?

--ooOoo--

Chapter 2

DRIFTING

THE COMMERCIAL WORLD

PA or Secretary?

Should I label myself as just a secretary or was I a personal assistant? A snag for future employment was that, as the job I had was with the Church, a charity, my interest in the position was considered to be a vocation. As I was still living at home, I was offered half the salary I could have achieved elsewhere. When eventually I moved to Cardiff to be closer to my fiancé who had moved to a new job, I was unable initially to commandeer a job of the calibre I thought I should be capable of. My previous salary on my CV was obviously uninspiring, and being secretary to a Bishop did not hold much weight in the world of commerce.

I ended up with a very menial job as Assistant Secretary in a car finance company which was part of a conglomerate merchant banking organisation housed in one building. It was a fledgling company - Hawtin and Partners, run by two ex-Julian Hodge employees. Julian Hodge was the Welsh financier of renown in the late '60s. Michael Kinane had been the Company Secretary and Freddie Hargreaves had been Julian Hodge's Personal Adviser.

Promotion or Demotion?

After three months in this very boring position in the car finance department, and not used to being told what to do by someone younger than myself, I was called into the office of these two senior directors. I wondered what misdemeanour I had committed and thought I was about to be sacked, or, at best, no longer needed. To my amazement, they had become out of favour, not with me, but with their Personal Assistant who was being demoted to the Bank below, and they wished me to take up the position. Whereas in the Bishop's employ I was passively more of a personal assistant/secretary, in this new role I had to take a very active role in decision-making on behalf of my new bosses, often running their office single-handedly during their frequent absences.

My position in this role, unfortunately, did not last long. After five months of marriage and two months into our new home, my husband was transferred to work as production manager in a factory in Widnes on Merseyside. I had worked for these two lovely guys for just under a year. Hawtin had a sister office in Liverpool and they managed to find a position there for me to transfer to. I worked partly in the accounts office, partly on the switchboard – in fact, it seemed they had literally granted the Cardiff office a favour and 'squeezed me in'. Once again, I was very bored as I didn't seem to have a tangible role. One of the highlights, as I remember, was being involved in what the Press referred to as 'The Nun's Story'.

A Love Story (not mine …)

There were three of us in the accounts office, Jane, Michael and myself. Michael had been a priest but had fallen in love with a nun whom he intended to marry. The only obstacle to the marriage was his dispensation from Rome which had not yet come through. He was desperately in love but wanted to do things in the right manner by the Church.

On one of Michael's days off, I happened to be doing a stint on the switchboard when I received a call from one of his golfing friends.

19

When this friend was told Michael was not at work he asked if I knew his home number. I thought this was a bit suspicious. Why phone his place of work to find his whereabouts on his day off? Surely he would know how to get in touch with him at home if he was a friend?

After a second of these calls, instinct told me these were possibly press scouts who had cottoned on to the unusual circumstances of Michael's romance and wanted a scoop. Luckily, I had had experience of the devious ways of the Press whilst working for the Bishop. Consequently, the Press learnt nothing from me. Regardless, they had somehow managed to catch up with Michael and Theresa who were enjoying a day out in the Cheshire countryside. How they managed to find them I know not, but pictures of them picnicking were splattered across the front page of the Liverpool Echo, and various other papers, under the heading "The Nun's Story".

New House, New Baby

My boredom in this job was not to last too long for, finally having sold our house in South Wales, and having bought one in Widnes, I became pregnant. The old saying "New house, new baby" rang very true because, by my calculations, our daughter, Michelle, must have been conceived the night we moved in!

I kept in touch with the office in Liverpool, and the Accounts Office in particular, after my baby was born. Michael and Theresa had finally become married, and Theresa, too, had become pregnant. But 'The Nun's Story' was to have a tragic end. Michael was experiencing bad stomach pains which turned out to be cancer.

Michael died a fortnight before his baby was born, and a few days before his first wedding anniversary. Theresa was heart-broken, and, to compound her grief, she took this event as God's punishment for having broken their vows. She had one consolation, she had a healthy baby who was a part of, and a reminder of, the man she so loved. I hope she has since learnt that God understands all and forgives.

Blessed Babes

I gave up work at Hawtin's in Liverpool a month before the expected birth date of my baby to give me time to decorate and prepare the nursery. However, life never seems to turn out as it should. The baby arrived early - two days after I left my employment.

Because our car had broken down, we had walked to and from evening Mass on All Saints' Day. Around midnight things started happening – my waters broke. We had not long been in the neighbourhood and knew no one we felt comfortable enough to call upon at that time of night, so my husband called an ambulance. Michelle was born 12 hours later, on All Souls' Day. Interestingly, some twenty months later, on Pentecost Sunday 1973, my son, Paul, was born, and my second daughter, Elisabeth, another 30 months on, was born on Good Friday 1976.

UNSETTLING TIMES

Nowhere to Live

Our start to married life had not been idyllic. During the first three and a quarter years we had lived at three temporary addresses and had moved into three different bought properties. The temporary addresses alone were quite some experience.

In March 1970, we had returned from honeymoon in Ireland only to find that the building society providing the mortgage for the house we were buying had not come up with the goods as expected. We should have been moving into our first home just outside Pontypridd, in a place named Church Village, but there was a further questionnaire to complete regarding the coal mining beneath the Rhonda Valley in which Ponty, and its surrounding area, nestles.

We had little option but to go cap-in-hand to the guys my husband had previously been sharing with, and they allowed us to have his old room for a week. Thereafter, they were moving out themselves and, as our house purchase was, by then, still not complete, my husband suggested we go to the terraced house in Maindy Road, Cardiff, where I had shared previously with three girls.

Four Females, One Male (Cardiff)

Very graciously, the girls agreed to us using their front room – it should have been just for a week or so. We used the mattress off the single bed from the twin room I had shared, plus the base cushions off the sofa - this acted as our marital bed. We 'existed' in this small living room, surrounded by what few possessions we owned, in this very small three bedroomed terrace, sharing kitchen and bathroom with three other female occupants who had forfeited their living room for our benefit - for the next seven weeks. This situation was quite difficult for us all, not least for my husband who was, at times, unable to contain his frustration. Unlike the very tolerant females in the household, his temper frequently became manifest, particularly behind closed doors.

The Rhonda Valley

Our accommodation problems did not much improve once we moved into our first home in Church Village in the Rhonda Valley. My husband lived there for only two months before he got transferred to Merseyside. I was left on my own to sell the house but at least I had our new cat for company - Tina, born in a manger at a local farm (my husband wanted to give her the Welsh name 'Myfanwy' but I objected – her nicknames alone could have left much to answer for!). After he moved, we took it in turn every weekend to visit each other

– I would take the train, travelling along the Welsh border up to Runcorn where he was lodging, and he would come down by car on the alternate weekends.

After three months of to-ing and fro-ing in this manner, we began to find it rather tiring. We had already spent almost every weekend at the beginning of the year travelling the country in a triangle – one weekend to my parents in Nottingham, and the other to his parents in Worthing – in our attempts to prepare for our wedding which took place in March of that year. Now winter was approaching. We decided I should move up to join him until the sale of our house in Wales was completed.

Runcorn, Merseyside

My husband found us a flat in Runcorn, the upper floor of a terrace property, across the road from the ICI Mond Division chemical works on the banks of the River Mersey. Obviously we had to be cautious about expenditure as we were still paying the mortgage on our first home, but at least we weren't paying the travelling costs each weekend, we were saving the wear and tear on ourselves – and we were together! This was, after all, still well within our first year of marriage. To be precise, we had had just eight months of married life – all very disrupted.

It was winter 1970/71. The flat was exceedingly damp. We had to keep two hot water bottles in the bed during the day to keep it aired and these were refilled to warm the bed at night, accompanied by Tina the cat for additional warmth - both for her benefit and for our's. Water ran down the walls. Fortunately, we went to family for Christmas, leaving Tina to be looked after by the family that had moved in downstairs.

Tina was not allowed out as she would no doubt stray across the road and would never be found if she wandered into the giant complex

23

that comprised the chemical works. Every evening, we would run a pyjama cord over the banister rail for her to chase up and down the stairs, and kick corks across the landing, to keep her entertained and exercised.

On our return from our three-day Christmas visit, we entered the dining room to find the floor covered in white, just like snow. We wondered what on earth had happened, only to discover that the poor cat, in between her play and feed-time downstairs, was so bored that she had shredded to a fine pulp a complete roll of kitchen towel we had left on the sideboard.

We remained in that flat from November until the beginning of February, and the damp and cold got no better as winter progressed. I was to experience my first memorable hoar frost whilst there. There seemed little point in moving as a house sale was in progress back in Wales and we had our house in Widnes lined up to move into as soon as the transactions were complete.

I have one good memory of the flat in Runcorn. We knew nobody in the area, and having just been away for Christmas, we decided the only way to spend New Year's Eve was to get tucked up in bed with the cat for company and warmth. I had been given a half bottle of whiskey and, together with a packet of nuts, we sat in bed feeling rather lonely, except for each other's company. Then, at midnight, something unexpected happened. There was a great cacophony as all the ships in the Mersey sounded their horns together to greet the New Year - we suddenly began to feel a reconnection with the world! It was quite a magical experience.

Widnes, Merseyside

We finally moved into our house in Widnes at the beginning of February 1971. It was not long before I realised I was pregnant, probably having conceived the day we moved in. A few months later, my husband was given notice and this time had no job to move to. His Father managed to pull a few strings and soon an interview awaited him in Sussex. It was a family-run joinery firm and they were prepared to wait until after the birth of our baby before requiring him to attend the interview as they wished to meet us as a family. This put a lot of pressure on him, particularly since, if he got the job, it would entail another move.

When she was four weeks old, and against recommendation from our health advisers, we took the baby down with us for the interview as my husband could wait no longer to know whether he had a job. This was very unsettling for the baby as she was struggling to breastfeed anyway because of the stress we were under. However, he was successful in achieving the post and was asked to start immediately. This time he had experienced nine months in the property.

There seemed to be a settled life ahead at last, except that, for a second time I was left to sell and pack up the house - and this time manage the new baby – entirely on my own. We had owned the house for just a year – somewhat of an improvement on the five months I had spent in our first home in Wales. My husband had only lived in that house for two months before his transfer to Merseyside.

Hurstpierpoint, Sussex

Eventually the house in Widnes sold and I moved to join my husband in a house I had never previously seen, into a village I had never heard of, Hurspierpoint in Sussex. Hurspierpoint nestled behind the South Downs, nine miles from Brighton. It was a very friendly, if somewhat up-market, neighbourhood, and the in-laws lived not far away in Worthing. We speedily settled in and began something of a social life for the first time after nearly two-and-a-half years as a married couple.

25

Once we had finally settled in Sussex, it was not long before I became pregnant again, with our son, Paul. This time I was working from home doing accounts and secretarial work for my husband, alongside being mother to our daughter, Michelle. I was beginning to enjoy the settled family life I had always craved. It had been far from settled to this point.

My husband's unpredictable violent tendencies, that began as soon as we returned from honeymoon, did not improve. I ended up one evening with a split head in a pool of blood as I fell against the dining table. The doctor who attended was a bit mystified but put it down to a dizzy spell caused by the pregnancy. My toddler daughter, at 15 months, witnessed the whole proceedings. I had put these violent episodes down to the unusual circumstances of our early married life and his recurring job losses which must, in his mind, have dented his image as provider. I put this latest episode down to stress at work.

Despite using me as an unpaid secretary, he was unable to make the company viable. Inevitably, he arrived home a few weeks later and announced he had been given notice – again. This must have been particularly embarrassing for him as it was a friend of his Father who had been persuaded that he would be the man for the job. We had been settled in this latest home for just 11 months and had finally unpacked the last of our wedding presents.

Norfolk

After another six months, when our son was nine weeks old, we set off for Norfolk. Having spent weeks of job-hunting, my husband was finally offered the management of a small joinery factory at Acle in Broadland, east Norfolk. We began house-hunting, starting from Great Yarmouth, and were horrified at the rather bleak small villages dotted about the Broadland area.

Every village seemed to comprise a main road named "The Street" with a few houses either side, and, if lucky, a shop and pub. The odd farmstead was to be found in between, as were churches, seemingly in the middle of nowhere. We came to learn these were known as "Black Death" churches because the plague of the 1300's had caused the villagers to die and their properties subsequently fell into ruin and became no more. When we moved to Norfolk it was the early 'seventies and some of the isolated marshland farms had no mains electricity. Even today, many properties still are not on main drains, and many villages do not have a gas supply despite the North Sea gas terminal at Bacton.

As we neared Norwich, prospects began to improve and we found a lovely house with a pine-clad interior in the very desirable and rather expensive area of Brundall, six miles east of Norwich. The upside of our enforced moves was that our initial nest-egg of £440 representing the 10% deposit that we had struggled to put together for our first home - just outside Pontypridd in the Welsh valleys in March 1970 – had incremented into a deposit enabling us to purchase this property at a price of £15,000 by July 1973, only three and a quarter years later.

DOWNHILL

The 'Episodes'

Once again I was doing secretarial work and acting as general dogsbody for the business my husband was running. The children invariably had to take second place as it was vital that this venture was a success after three of my husband's career failures to date. Not only was his career important to him, but particularly to me as I saw his success as being the key to the cessation of his violent episodes. These continued, always unpredictable, and not always directed at

27

me but at the house, too, which was becoming increasingly wrecked. Holes appeared in doors which were sometimes replaced (he was a joiner after all) but with no time for them to be redecorated. Objects were thrown against walls which often retained, long term, the evidence of their destruction.

Sometimes these violent episodes had a humorous side to them in retrospect, such as the time when we were expecting guests for dinner and he threw a saucepan across the kitchen which knocked the knob off the eye-level oven door. The guests were ten minutes away from arriving and the oven contained the casserole we were due to be sharing with them. Fortunately, a pair of pliers saved the evening. Not so humorous was the time he wrenched the radiator from the bathroom wall with the consequence that water poured through the kitchen ceiling. I forget the outcome of that episode.

As soon as the bouts were over, so were the black moods that triggered them, and he carried on as though nothing had happened - despite the devastation. He would appear completely surprised when I was unable to share in his recovered conviviality, seeming totally unaware of my battered and bruised body that prevented me from recovering mine.

Receivership

Everything seemed about to come crashing down again business-wise, just as I became unexpectedly pregnant with our third child, Elisabeth. The business he was working for went into receivership and a house move seemed likely to be on the cards yet again – always, it seemed, around the time of a birth of one of the children.

At this stage, his parents were becoming increasingly anxious about this eldest son of theirs who seemed to be totally dogged by bad luck. Eventually, a plan was devised for when the assets of the business being liquidated came up for sale. He, his parents, and his middle brother, who was also out of work at this time, decided to buy up the assets of the failed business and form a company of their own to continue with the order book as it stood.

Thus began the building up of a new, reformed, joinery business. My husband was to be the Managing Director, his brother the Company Secretary, and their Mother a third director. Their Father, having his own architectural practice, decided it was imprudent to be involved but put up the majority share of the money with an indirect interest via his wife.

The business was almost doomed to failure from the start. His brother did not pull his weight, having very little knowledge of business, particularly joinery, and the brothers fell out in a big way. My husband continued on his own, having also out-manoeuvred his Mother by getting her to sign away her interest in the business in a surreptitious manner so that she did not realise what she was doing.

Middle Eastern Madness

All went well for a while until my husband was approached by a Middle Eastern organisation that offered him a big contract for the manufacture of large television cabinets for wealthy Asians. It meant putting 80% of production towards this contract and I had a very uneasy feeling about it. It was not so much about the 80% of investment being placed toward the one contract, though this did not seem like good business practice; it was merely a gut feeling. Some would call it a feminine sixth sense.

Although I voiced my concerns, my opinion held no weight in the business – I was merely the very overworked secretary and general dogsbody, trying to juggle three children under the age of five and a very unpredictable husband who would also expect me to drop everything to carry out some 'urgent' errand for the business (and would I dare say "No"?). I was rapidly running out of energy. Also during this time, he had the opportunity to have a ground-breaking operation on his ear-drum that had been perforated since the age of three. Two of his middle ear ossicles were to be replaced after years of damage due to infection and his ear drum sealed up with a skin graft. While he was in hospital I had to run his business as best I could, look after the three children, and make regular hospital visits to see how he was, and keep him updated on business affairs.

The Middle Eastern company turned out to be crooked and pulled the plug on the contract mid-way through. The QC who had given us a reference for the company proved to have no influence on the outcome – in fact, we even heard that unwanted personnel connected with this middle-eastern company had been 'disposed' of. My husband's company was on the verge of bankruptcy. Father-in-law had lost his investment anyway.

An Insight

My deep relationship with God had somewhat waned by this time – there seemed hardly enough time to breathe, let alone pray. In fact, it began to wane early in the marriage as it is not easy being intimately in love with two persons at once. Before marriage there was only God; afterwards, my time and thoughts had to be shared between Him and my husband. One inevitably gained priority. Unfortunately, my husband's nature meant that the priority fell with him – he took up all my time and energy. This experience provided me with a great insight into the value of celibacy for those for whom the choice is right.

~

REFLECTION:

ABANDONMENT

Looking back, for the first three and a half years of married life, and the handful of months before, we seemed, as a couple, like nomads drifting in a desert. We had a goal: to achieve a home for a family with a decent income to support it, but the path to getting there seemed to have no rhyme or reason. It reminds me of the Israelites of the Old Testament trying to reach the Promised Land, wandering around in the desert because they kept losing their focus – on God who was their protector and leader.

My focus was not where it should have been because of the busyness of what we seemed to be perpetually engaged in: moving to and from temporary accommodation, buying and selling houses, packing and unpacking our possessions, constantly chasing after new jobs, working above average hours - and children. There were dangers around, too, to which I fell prey, and I sometimes wondered why this God of mine allowed such things to happen.

Then years later I was given a copy of the poem 'Footsteps'. I had been aware of God by my side through most of my life prior to marriage, and, as per the poem, there had been two sets of footsteps in the sand through which I had metaphorically walked, the second belonging to the Lord. When I subsequently became aware of only one set of prints, ie when I felt God had not been there for me during my marriage (and I must admit to having all but neglected Him, so maybe I was getting my just dues?), I realised He had not abandoned me at all. On the contrary, the one set of footprints during the difficult times were not, as one is apt to assume, one's own footsteps. I came to realise that these steps were far too large to be mine - the footprints were the Lord's, for, in His infinite love, He was carrying me when times were hardest.

31

It is easy to think that because we have not always been faithful to Him that God will neglect us in turn. 'An eye for an eye' only features in the human condition and Jesus taught that we should be far more God-like and generous in our behaviour than meting out like-for-like. (Matt 5:38-42).

THOUGHTS FOR DISCUSSION

1. Earthly life is full of difficulties, but being aware that God is around, supporting and loving us, makes problems and trials easier to bear. Can you imagine what life might be like without God's loving support?

2. How aware are you that God is constantly present in your life regardless of where you are at, or what attention you pay Him?

3. What do you think happens when we turn away from God and His teachings?

--ooOoo--

Chapter 3

TRANSFORMATION

BREAKDOWN/BREAKUP

Dutch Friends

I had become very friendly with a Dutch family that I had met at the school gate. It was 1979 and Michelle and Paul were attending the local Primary School. As a family, we had a lot in common in that their three girls were of similar age to my three children, and they had a Belgian au-pair. My Mother was a French-speaking Belgian - her second language, Flemish, being a derivation of Dutch – some would even say a corruption. There are those, particularly the Dutch themselves, who consider it a slang version of their language and barbed jokes about the Flemings abound. Christine was in fact a Scot with a legal degree and fluent in five languages. Her husband, Frans, was an industrial psychologist.

We shared a lot of time together over the children, and Christine and I enjoyed walking and the occasional day out at weekends. Their home, a large Victorian property with an equally sizeable garden, was a haven of peace and tranquillity, reminding me of idyllic childhood days spent at my English Grandparents' home where we went regularly for tea. I was always saddened to think that I didn't have time to sit and relax with Frans and Christine over the glass of wine offered whenever it was my turn to fetch our children home from School.

Frans had obviously spotted that I was in some sort of difficulty and assumed there were marital issues which I flatly denied. There had been periods of up to nine months between the bouts of violence when everything was fine. I assured Frans it was purely temporary; we were under strain because of my husband's business difficulties. Once he got his business sorted and successful, then things would be easier.

Breakdown

One afternoon, just before my Mother was due to arrive for the weekend, I was trying to type a business letter, the body of which was a mere two or three lines. My concentration had become so poor it took me over two hours. I ended up in bed and didn't get up as my brain seemed to have given up the ghost. Because of my Dutch friends - my allies, and my Mother's presence, albeit only for the weekend - I felt relatively safe to do this even knowing my husband would not be pleased. Not that I had much capability to do otherwise...

What occurred during the next 12 – 18 months is a story in itself. Suffice it to say it was a wake-up call. I had finally given way to what was complete nervous exhaustion culminating in a breakdown. During this period our Dutch friends took me and the children under their wing, allowing us to stay under their roof until I had recovered some equilibrium. I was assured that had this not happened, and if I did not eat properly, I would have ended up in the local Hellesdon Hospital for the mentally ill. I am convinced that my current obesity results from this threat regarding not eating sufficiently as nowadays I over-compensate!

The last Straw

Once recovered sufficiently I decided to return home. Now that my husband's violence was out in the open, surely he would not dare to harm me again? I decided to give him another chance. Everything seemed to go reasonably well until one day, almost a year later, we were returning from a very enjoyable family day out. On the way home, he said he needed to stop to see somebody connected with work. I merely asked out of interest, having been previously involved very closely with his business, what he needed to see this person about. I was answered by a swipe across my face which resulted in a serious nose bleed and a broken nose.

Whether he so despaired that he had failed again, or what, I do not know, but he drove like a maniac, zigzagging the car across the roads until we were out in open country where he turned the car at speed into a field, damaging the undercarriage. The children were terrified but fortunately unharmed. Apparently, the reason for the outburst was that he was feeling sensitive because he owed money to the person I had, in all innocence, asked about. Life was becoming far too dangerous.

The children were becoming more aware, too, and I came to realise I had no chance of full recovery from my breakdown and depression whilst I continued to live with him. I also came to the realisation that, for all our sakes, to continue living with him under current circumstances was far too risky. I opted for a Separation Order. I was in no state to make the momentous decision of obtaining a divorce, though this, almost inevitably, was to come later.

Discombobulation

The decision, when it came, was a hard one. Divorce was something I could not easily take on board as I had taken a vow at marriage 'until death do us part'. I had always believed marriage was for life and I wanted it to be for life. I still loved my husband for himself but his unpredictable, erratic, violent behaviour was far too dangerous to live with. It also caused me a crisis of faith. I sometimes wonder how much this dichotomy with my belief system was an exacerbating cause of my breakdown. The inevitability of divorce made me feel as if the rug had been pulled completely from under the whole of my belief system. It felt as though a blunderbuss had blown through my soul.

My second dilemma was, how was I going to cope with three children on my own, aged between three and eight, and no means of earning an income? I had visions of being forever at the bottom end of the social spectrum which did not sit well with the lifestyle I had been accustomed to in my childhood. I had visions of ending up in social housing – at the time these were post-war pre-fabricated units on the old airport estate in Fifers Lane, Norwich. We would lose our friends and the familiarity of school, doctors, etc. There was also the fear that, whilst I was behind my husband, helping and supporting him, his outbursts had been bad enough. Divorcing him would inflame him and what effect would that have on his anger and any consequent violence? I had struck rock bottom and could see no way up or out.

Penury

What was I to do to make life worthwhile? I had had every ounce of confidence knocked out of me - literally. I had very little energy and I dreaded what the 'Ex' might do. He was so clever, I imagined that he might make out I was too mentally unstable to be capable of managing the children and they would be taken away. I seriously feared he might come with a shotgun and do us all in. People were telling me things would get better – I just couldn't believe it.

My faith in God had been shattered – my naive idea about Him was that, if I prayed hard enough He would sort out the marriage because, after all, isn't that what He wants – for marriage to be a vehicle for love, for life? But He didn't sort it out. He had let me down big time. Maybe I hadn't prayed hard enough?

I still believed in God – after the first-hand encounter I had experienced in my 'teens I don't think I could ever not believe in Him again. But I was disillusioned and very, very angry with Him. Some time later, a very wise priest told me that to be angry with God was a healthy sign because it meant there was still a relationship. Otherwise I would not have cared. But the relationship at the time seemed no more than the equivalent of trying to talk to someone on the phone and receiving only heavy breathing in return – I knew He was there but He seemed not to be responding. Then later in life I experienced a shocking enlightenment: if I was angry with God I was putting myself above Him, in that what I was telling God is that I knew better than He what was good for me.

Fighting for Pennies

The humiliation of applying for Social Security benefits had at least the upside of providing a means of feeding ourselves. I had been granted maintenance of £3.00 per week per child (and 0.5p per year for myself!) on the basis that my ex-husband was unable to afford more. Three weeks after being given this Order by the Court, he managed to acquire a mortgage for a prestige three-bedroomed flat in the smart, redeveloped, old brewery building at Anchor Quay in Norwich where he became the first resident. Very soon after, the maintenance payments dried up.

There followed years of having to take him to Court because the Social Security was not prepared to pay out unless they had proof that he could not afford to pay the maintenance himself. The downside of this was that the Social Security would not apply to the Courts themselves; it had to be done by the Benefit applicant. Thus, I was branded as 'the aggressor' by my Ex which he ensured was made common knowledge, including to the children who were too young to understand the implications that, with neither maintenance nor Benefits, there would be no money for food, clothes or the roof over our heads. The 'Social' paid the interest element of the mortgage, but even when the children had all become teenagers at the end of the 'Eighties, the total weekly amount I was receiving, including for the mortgage, was just less than £115 per week.

ADVENTURES

Car Crisis

The first thing I did, once I began recovering from my breakdown, was to search for a part-time job that fitted in with School hours. I was permitted to earn up to £15 per week under Social Security rules at the time. I did some cleaning jobs and eventually began selling Usbourne books on a party-plan basis. Living in a rural village this required a car. Fortunately, I had this ancient car that at least got me from A to B so long as I could judge the petrol consumption as the fuel gauge, among other minor bits, did not work.

One day, when the children were at school, I received an unexpected visit from my ex-husband. He engaged me in conversation on the doorstep and then suddenly stepped inside and grabbed the car keys that were hanging on a key rack just inside the hall. I never saw the car again. This left me in a dilemma as I had some book parties planned and no means of getting to them.

One of my friends in the village, on hearing of my predicament, had a chat with her husband and, much to my surprise, offered me the use of their old car. This was an old Wolseley 1880 that had sat in their drive for well over a year. It had been their family car during the time their children were young. When they upgraded to a newer model, they could not bear to part with the Wolseley for all the memories it held. They told me I could have it if it was any use, but it needed a little money spending on it.

The car repairs cost me less than I might have spent on some other, cheap, second-hand, and possibly unreliable model. I could not afford to repair the power-assisted steering that had failed so it was very heavy to drive, but it did mean I could carry on my new-found work and generally keep the family running in a near normal manner.

Fire!

We had many exciting times in this old vehicle - which is maybe why it earned the name Chitty Bang Bang after the film of similar title - and some close scrapes. Coming through the centre of Norwich one winter Sunday evening, on our return from Mass at the Cathedral, we were travelling down Guildhall Hill when suddenly the headlights failed and the car came to a halt. Then I saw smoke coming from the engine. I yelled to the children to get out of the car quickly and grabbed the little fire extinguisher which I had inherited with the car - but it did not work.

Behind us was a caravette, the owner of which realised what was happening and appeared with a fully working, larger extinguisher than the little hand-held, useless one I had. The fire was duly extinguished. It turned out to be a relatively minor problem; whoever had serviced the car a day or two earlier had not replaced one of the battery terminals properly and it had caused a short.

Precious Cargo

Hills are quite rare in Norfolk but a second, fairly major incident occurred on another one some time later - on Ketts Hill in Norwich. I was returning from Norwich in time to pick up the children from school. Nearly at the summit of the hill, just past the Prison, I had to pull out to overtake a cyclist. As I did so I suddenly felt a crunch and scrape and realised something was seriously wrong. I got out of the car and found the front offside wheel lying at an angle to the car. As the thought went through my mind "What on earth am I going to do now?" two policemen appeared at my side. Apparently they had just dropped off a couple of prisoners at the jail and were travelling directly behind me. Who says Guardian Angels don't exist?!

One policeman took over the traffic control and the other took me to the pavement at the side of the road.

"OK," he said, "Let's contact your husband for you."
"I haven't got one."
"Are you a member of the RAC or AA?"
"No."
"Where is your garage?"
"I don't have a particular one."
"Right," he said, "We'll have to get a pick-up vehicle to tow it away."
"How am I going to get home?"
"You'll have to get a taxi."
I was already very concerned about whether the car was repairable, let alone what it would cost if it was. On top of this, paying for a taxi was something out of my league. My more immediate concern was the children. The policeman suggested I ask in the shop if they would allow me to make a phone call. A small bonus in my otherwise unlucky day was that the shop owner refused my offer of payment. I rang a friend who said she would pick up the children for me and deposit them with my neighbour. I then rang my neighbour, Mabel, an elderly lady who was like a third Grandma to my children, to tell her what was happening and ask if she would mind the children until I got back.

It was then I remembered I had this neighbour's shopping in the car – two bottles of Claymore Whiskey. She would crucify me if I returned home without her precious shopping. I didn't cotton on until years later that she was not just agoraphobic but an alcoholic also. My dilemma was, how was I to retrieve from the car these two bottles that had been rolling around in the footwell, from a car that was now stuck in the middle of a busy road with a policeman hovering over it?

As the lesser of two evils, I plucked up the courage and told the policeman with me that I had some things in the car that I would need if the car was to be towed away. He advised me to get into the car and shut the door behind me. Luckily I found a carrier bag and stuffed everything I needed into it, including the two items of precious cargo.

Citizens Band

I did not learn till later that evening that my incident had been the cause of major interest around the county. I was due to go out with a new friend who, by coincidence, was picking me up from home – usually such meetings were arranged on neutral ground. Mabel, my agoraphobic and whiskey-loving neighbour, always did the 'babysitting'. She loved the company and refused any offer of money so long as I shared a glass of whiskey with her at the end of the evening.

When I told this new friend how fortuitous it was that he was collecting me from home, and related to him the events of the day, he said: "Gosh, it was YOU who was at the centre of events this afternoon!" It turned out he was a Citizens Band enthusiast. He was approaching St Williams Way, a couple of roads away from Ketts Hill, when the report of an incident came through. He was in contact with an articulated lorry, the driver of which was worried he might not be able to get down Ketts Hill past the obstruction. My friend told him he would go down and check out the situation. The message back was that he had better search for a different route into the City as the broken-down car lay straddled almost in the middle of the road. "They won't believe it tomorrow when I tell them I dated the girl at the centre of the incident!" 'Them', of course, being his fellow CB enthusiasts.

Nasty Noises

Once the axle had been repaired the car was soon back in use. Some weeks later I was taking the children to school, and this elderly neighbour to the local minimarket to get her shopping, no doubt to include two more bottles of whiskey. As I tried to reverse out of our parking space a very weird grinding noise came from the car and I eased it back into the parking slot and said we would have to walk. Mabel was furious. "You promised to take me shopping!" she yelled. "But I daren't use the car until I have had it checked out to find out what is wrong!" and I reminded her of what had happened a few weeks earlier. She was not easily appeased.

Rocky Road

Adventures in Chitty never ceased to surprise. I was returning from a book demo in Spixworth via the shortcut of Stonehouse Road, a rather narrow, winding lane and not a priority on the Council's repair list. As I was nearing the B1140 from Wroxham to Salhouse there was a noise under the car. I assumed, from what I saw in the rear mirror, that I had scraped over a sugar beet that had dropped off the back of one of the collection lorries on its way to the British Sugar factory at Cantley. These Wolsey's had very low-slung engines.

As I continued to drive, I happened to notice that the oil gauge needle was plummeting. I knew this was serious and the nearest safe place to park was by the entrance to Salhouse Church. "That was no sugar beet" said the mechanic who had come out from a nearby garage at the request of a passer-by who had stopped to see if he could help. "It must have been a rock to cause such damage. You've wrecked the oil sump – it will mean a new engine." Having towed Chitty to his Garage, he drove me home. I was in somewhat of a state of shock so told him I would think about a replacement engine once I had an estimate of the cost.

Having recovered my wits somewhat, I decided I ought to alert the Police with the purpose of getting the offending rock removed before it caused damage to other road-users. After spending some time trying to define the exact location of the accident to be able to pass the incident to the appropriate Police area for attention, the duty Sergeant eventually asked: "Madam, what exactly is it you want us to do?" I told him what had happened to me and said I thought it would be appropriate for someone to go and remove the rock. He replied: "Madam, do you realise that if I make a report of this incident you could be fined for driving without due care and attention?"

I was flabbergasted. Apparently, the area was at the crossroads of four different Police responsibilities and he obviously did not want to spend any more time trying to work out which one applied. I subsequently learnt that if the Police make a report of an incident they are then duty-bound to resolve the issue and, what to me had been a major incident, to them was a minor one. It was hardly the response one expected to hear, though, when attempting to be a socially responsible citizen.

The trail of oil that emerged from Stonehouse Road all the way to Salhouse Church was visible for all to see, and remained as a reminder of my crisis until the road was resurfaced some eighteen months later.

SAMARITANS

Steps forward

Selling books was an easing into increasing my confidence so badly shattered over the years, and I did this alongside the cleaning jobs. I also wanted to do something to repay my friends who had been so helpful and supportive throughout my crisis. They had everything -

good health, money, a comfortable life-style. Little was I to know what would happen to them in years to come. There seemed no way I could help them other than by trying to fully regain my health. Then one day I had an inspiration. With trepidation, I applied to join the Samaritans. It seemed to me the best repayment was to attempt to do for others what these friends had done for me.

I did not realise what a complex system of scrutiny was involved in choosing suitable applicants to become Samaritans, but rightly so. After an intense day of talks, questions and role plays, we were told that only approximately 30% of applicants succeeded. I was still quite depressed and I felt certain this was apparent to these scrutineers whose purpose, in the main, was to help people such as myself. I thought I would be found out for what I was - more a client than a potential helper.

Later that day occurred one of the biggest turning points for the rebuilding of my confidence - the phone call to say that I was one of the few that had been chosen. I was elated! It was early 1981. It was the first boost to my badly shattered morale and the first step towards a more wholesome future. And I loved the work.

The Manual

As part of our training, we were given a manual to read outlining the various conditions, and the symptoms indicating them, that we were likely to encounter during our work as Samaritans. A chapter that intrigued me particularly was the one on psychopathy.

As I digested the various symptoms concerning this particular disorder from the manual, I became rather stunned by what I was reading. My ex-husband qualified outright in eight of the eleven indicators. Only one was required to qualify as a psychopath. However, as there had been no official diagnosis to this effect I kept my discovery to myself. Besides, some might think it was merely

44

'sour grapes' to justify my divorce as the symptoms would not necessarily have been apparent to those who did not know him well. However, the discovery did make me feel a little more justified about what I had had to cope with during our marriage.

Some years later, a social worker, who was liaising with the children's Father because of their reluctance to visit him, gave me some useful advice. She said I had to treat him as a fourth child, and in the next breath she told me something that changed my outlook on the years of my marriage forever. She stated that he had been labelled a 'borderline psychopath'. To hear this being confirmed in an official capacity was a burden lifted from my shoulders for ever. I was finally absolved from the guilt I had carried over the years thinking that I had somehow, in deed or personality, inadvertently triggered his violent episodes.

Philip – The Samaritan

At Samaritans, I was assigned a Mentor who was a delightful, slightly physically impaired, academic - an art historian named Philip. In the few quiet times between managing phone calls and the visitors to the Centre, we would chat. We were usually three persons on a duty rota for a period of 3.5 hours which gave us a good chance to get to know each other when things were not busy.

Philip was full of wisdom, and when he realised my problems regarding my earning capacity, he made what, at the time, seemed a bizarre suggestion: "Why don't you go to university and get a degree?"

The idea of university had appealed in my youth in principle, but my shyness and naivety at the time had been one of the main hindrances to my going. Also, as a teenager, I had not been able to decide on which of many career choices to plump for and this was important in defining which subjects to take at 'A' Levels, let alone University.

Then there was my Father who was less than encouraging. Being a non-academic himself, he was very much of the mind that, as he had paid for our education up to the age of 16 ('O' Level standard), he had done his bit - there were six of us to consider. So little encouragement there. I am fairly sure, had I had a serious intent to pursue a subject at University, he might have relented. But he had this idea of fairness that, if he paid for my further education, there would be five more of his progeny he would feel duty-bound to treat equally so there would have been serious consequences to his pocket. He was also quite Victorian in his outlook and was of a mind that university was likely to be wasted on a girl as her main purpose in life should be marriage and children. So I didn't go to university, and I didn't do 'A' Levels.

Academia

The idea of stretching my mind quite appealed, particularly after years of being immersed in the not-so-mind-enlarging occupation of child-rearing. However, the biggest obstacle seemed to me to be the lack of these 'A' levels. This was the beginning of the 1980's and unbeknown to me, but not to Philip who was still attached to the local University of East Anglia, the University was a forerunner in encouraging 'mature' students.

"I am sure you have the ability," said Philip. "I will sponsor you. You will probably need to write a couple of papers but I am sure you are capable." Another guy who often shared a duty with us was a journalist, and between the pair of them I was given tips on essay writing and learnt how to 'cut and paste' essays in the good old-fashioned way. (Common-use computers were still a twinkle in the eye of Ian Sinclair and his forerunners).

46

Paul - The Rebel

Another problem resultant from my single parent status was a son with no male role model. He was a very bright child who did not mix with his contemporaries. We discovered, some years later, that he found their company less than stimulating because he had a brain that was three years ahead of his standard academic year. Consequently, he was incredibly difficult to handle particularly as he was very bored at his primary school.

His behaviour, at times, bordered on delinquency – a bright, unstretched mind will be put to use manufacturing mischief if there is nothing more stimulating on which to exercise it. My Father found him a challenge and a worry on our visits to the Midlands, and he was constantly chastising him for the slightest misdemeanour which simply aggravated Paul's behaviour. At home, he was surrounded by females; his two sisters, me, our elderly neighbour, Mabel, who was our baby-sitter and third Granny – even the pet cats were both female.

Joy – another Samaritan

Another person who often formed the duty trio with me at Samaritans, was a lovely lady, who, I later learnt, was the wife of the Head Master of the Norwich School. When she heard of my problems with Paul, she suggested I entered him for the School as she felt the academic level would serve him more adequately than the local comprehensive where he was soon scheduled to go. She obviously did not realise I was in receipt of Benefits and there was no way I could afford the fees.

The Norwich School was very proud of its sporting heritage, and had a special focus on the arts and music, and there were scholarships available. My son was neither sporty nor musical – apart from once taking our piano to bits to discover how it worked (and then losing interest before reassembling it) - nor was he interested in the arts, so a scholarship seemed out of the question. Apparently, there were also Government Assisted Places of which six were awarded each year. Depending on the parent's level of income, the Government would pay the balance of the fees.

Paul was entered for the exam. He was not very keen on the idea of going to this school so did not give of his best in the exam. He came seventh. I was very disappointed. On my next duty with Joy I told her the news. She told me not to worry – many boys were entered for the exams of various public schools and they then chose their preferred offer. She was right and, being top of the waiting list, Paul was eventually summoned for an interview.

The Enigma

I had my doubts that Paul would achieve a place because he did not identify with any of the School's ideals. However, having regaled the Head Master with the intriguing life history and antics of his pet hamster (as the Head informed us afterwards) the Head deemed him interesting enough to be granted a place. He had astutely picked up on Paul's reticence towards gregariousness and suggested he might be more interested in solo sports such as canoeing.

Sport did not feature in Paul's life at all during his school years, not even regarding canoeing. Life changed for him in more ways than one when he met Sarah, his wife-to-be, at age 16. His voice had broken only a year earlier. She was training to become a junior school teacher, specialising in outward-bound studies. Climbing and running were their first interests as a couple, followed by mountain biking. I bought them climbing gear as a wedding present to ensure their safety.

It was not long before Paul reached the higher echelons of amateur mountain biking and regularly took part in triathlons and other races. Three times he won the 24-hour Solo Marathon on his mountain bike out of a total of seven attempts. He was forever trialling and winning bike frames and parts, and other sundry trophies and goodies. At the Norwich School his sporting attempts manifested as comedy acts on the playing fields at which even his sports teacher could not help but be amused.

Life was beginning to turn a corner…..

~

REFLECTION:

PRIDE & WORRY:

In 1978, when I was first considering what I should do to escape my husband's unpredictable and increasing violence, I didn't know where to turn. I was too proud to admit to my family the problems I was having. The Church had not yet taken fully on board how to minister to those with breaking, or broken marriages; Woman's Refuges, at the time, were quite innovative and, anyway, seemed to be 'not for the likes of us'. My pride precluded me from seeking help. Help, in the end, found me.

I tried to hang on to my pride to the point where both my body and mind gave out. In the end, I lost everything – our lovely home, the image of the perfect family I craved, our future as once I had dreamt it would be. Instead, I became the penniless mother of three, a single parent, potential divorcee, and status-less. What would have happened had I turned to my parents?

When, finally, I sank beneath the waves, my pride stripped from me and my ego laid bare, thankfully I had friends who stood by. There were those who took me and the children under their roof when I could no longer cope, those who organised a solicitor, those who, when the chips were down, provided me with a means of transport and asked no recompense, and those who came with mops and buckets to sort out the house we needed to move into. We were able to stay in our own community, the children remaining at their schools, all thanks, in no small part, to our good Christian friends. God provides, whether we worry or not. (Matt 6:28-34)

With my ego stripped I could rebuild my life with values that truly mattered. I had the opportunity to change. Change normally refers to new beginnings. In some ways, what I experienced was deeper than change – it was a transformation, which more often happens after something old falls apart. The falling apart, the chaos, invites the soul to listen at a deeper level. It sometimes forces one to go to a new place because the old one is destroyed. I had to rebuild the whole of my belief system but this time from my own logic and personal understanding. And worry is something that has very little effect, if any, on me nowadays because I learnt that it achieves nothing and changes nothing - except the effect on one's health, and can therefore be a bother to others around us too.

THOUGHTS FOR DISCUSSION

1. Why is personal change difficult without some external intervening force or forces?

2. When going through a bad patch, how aware have you been of 'good Samaritans' around you?

3. Who do you suppose was responsible for placing these 'good Samaritans' in the right place to help you when needed?

--ooOoo--

Chapter 4

NEW BEGINNINGS

1984

Changes

Both Paul and I began our new academic experiences in the same year, 1984. I had passed too, and gained my university place with my entry essay on the philosophical subject of free will and determinism. As is typical of my nature, a procrastinator, I sat on the fence and argued for both sides, allowing that we appeared to have free will, but that there was an element of determinism in life caused by factors beyond our control - God being the Author of all destiny. I shall never forget the pride I felt on the first day, as I rolled up University Drive in my tatty old car, which, for once, thankfully did not appear out of place in the student car park.

With sadness, I gave up my role as a Samaritan just as I was being approached with the accolade that the Steering Group wished me to become a Leader. A week or two earlier, I had experienced a very heavy face-to-face case with which I had to deal, and which I managed to help turn around – for the time being at least. It was rare to hear how clients progressed after their presenting crisis - except in the case of the 'regulars'. These were foot-fetishers, kleptomaniacs, the odd paedophile, street walkers, etc. who rang in frequently. There were also those who lived on the streets, or in hostels who were turned out during the day, and they would come into the Centre for warmth, a cup of tea and a sympathetic ear. By allowing them to talk, particularly if we were experiencing a lull in activities, we were at least keeping them from being a possible nuisance to the public. I felt particularly sorry for the homosexuals, transsexuals, etc - they were still much ostracised in the early 'eighties, even by their families, to the point where they often became very depressed and often suicidal.

I must have come out of the interview room that day looking very drained, because my duty co-workers rallied around and encouraged me to off-load, as was the norm in such situations. We could share with our fellow Samaritans but there was a strict code of confidentiality concerning discussion of cases elsewhere.

So, as much as I loved the work and found it so very rewarding, I had to leave. As a single parent with children whose ages still ranged from only eight to thirteen, I was to have a large enough task on my hands taking on a full-time degree, albeit with only 8.5 hours of course lectures per week - or 'contact hours' as they were referred to in academic circles.

I felt my life beginning to turn. The bleak future I had foreseen in the depths of my depression somehow seemed to be brightening – as people had said it would.

Autumn 1984

Autumn of 1984 was therefore a very exciting time and proved to be a great milestone in our lives as a family. Paul set off reluctantly, but intrigued, in September to start the term at his new school. His behaviour began to settle as his mind became more stretched academically, leaving less time for boredom. He was now in an environment of male role models he could respect, something he had missed for most of his earlier life.

I, with an overwhelming feeling of pride and excitement, drove up to the University in October to begin a completely new life. It seemed inconceivable that this shy, retiring, unconfident person that had been me, would now be mixing with qualified academics, some of whom were of a similar age to me. It seemed, also, a step in the right direction in getting us re-established as a family with something of a social status. Divorce was still very much the exception in the 'seventies and early 'eighties and, as a woman with no career, no husband and no money, there was no status – a sense of nothingness in terms of where one fitted in the social scheme of things. People found it difficult to look on you other then as some sort of failure – or at least that was how it felt.

Even the Church was little equipped to offer support at the time, despite the Catholic Marriage counsellors being completely against the marriage continuing - given the circumstances. I had been told that I had a 'high ideal' of marriage and, at some point, I was asked, rather shockingly it seemed at the time, why I hadn't stuck a knife in his back? Perhaps they were just looking for a reaction as I was still in a numbed state at the time.

However, I was now on my way to achieving recognisable academic status, with a son whose academic abilities had already been recognised by his acceptance at one of the top public schools in the country.

The Gifted One

Even my eldest, Michelle, now at the Notre Dame High School, who had struggled academically throughout her school life, began to feel the influence of the academic atmosphere of the household as we all did our homework together. She began to improve her performance and gradually crept up through the streams. As the eldest, her earlier schooling had been so profoundly affected by the family problems. Even when at Nursery School, I remember picking her up at the end of a morning, and being told, most times, that she had had a good sleep in the arms of the lovely plump lady assistant. My thoughts were, why are we paying for her to attend Nursery, only for her to fall asleep?

In retrospect, I believe she was very stressed by the goings-on at home. Nursery School, for her, was a haven of peace where she could relax. After the separation, I attended a Primary School parents' evening and spoke to her form teacher who claimed that Michelle had been doing much better in recent weeks. I assumed the Head had told her of the changed family circumstances, but apparently he had not. "Oh, that will account for the difference in her!" she exclaimed. "Previously Michelle went around as though she had the whole world's problems on her shoulders. Now she seems so much more carefree." Little had we, as parents, realised how much the adverse home circumstances were affecting her – more to the point, we had not had time to be fully aware. I hadn't even noticed the negative build-up it had been having on me either, until it was too late.

Michelle was always conscious of, and felt very keenly, the better academic abilities of her younger siblings. Her great asset was that she was gifted with a sensitivity and understanding of babies and young children, and she had wanted to become a Nursery Nurse or Nanny from a very early age. I tried to assure her that this gift of hers was exceptional and she should concentrate on that asset rather than worry herself with thoughts that she was, or would be, in any way less valued then her younger brother or sister.

Subject Matter

My chosen subjects at UEA were Linguistics and Philosophy. The ten years of experience I gained from trying to analyse and understand my husband's behaviour caused me to have a preference to study psychology, but regrettably the UEA had no psychology department at that time. Before marriage, my contemporaries would often seek me out with their problems and I enjoyed trying to help them. My inclination was to become a Counsellor, and my time with the Samaritans had confirmed this, though Samaritan work is not exactly counselling but listening. The type of Counselling I was interested in was Person-Centred, promoted by Carl Rogers, whereby one also mainly listens with an empathetic ear and, quite often, the counselee, by talking out their concerns, will come to see the answer to their own problems.

My best choice of subject, therefore, was to choose mainly the semantic-based subjects in linguistics, with the addition of philosophy. These seemed to be good general subjects for aiding the understanding, at least in part, of the human mind. As mine was a combined study programme it straddled two of the University's schools – The School of Social Studies (SOC) in which was embedded the teaching of philosophy, and the School of English and American Studies (EAS) for linguistics. I was registered in the former.

If I had had free choice of subjects, I would have probably followed the Writing Course in EAS. I could not afford to pursue this path at this juncture because of the need to ensure the strongest possibility of an immediate income. I also felt I would have had more in common with the students in this School because of my interest in writing and literature. There have been some very interesting alumni, both lecturers and writers, past and current, such as Malcolm Bradbury, Ian McKewan, Rose Tremain, Kasuo Ishiguru, Lorna Sage, and her husband, Vic, who was Dean of the School at the time I was there. However, this was a dream for the future. It was probably a fortuitous that I was based in SOC as the sociology influence of being attached to this School rubbed off in a positive way on what was ultimately to become my career.

Mature Students

Life at Uni as a mature student was probably more enjoyable than having come straight from school. Quite often, young students arrive at university almost burnt out from the years of intense study for their GCSEs and 'A' levels. I could begin to appreciate the need for students to experience a Gap Year which, up to that point, I had considered to be something of an indulgence. For me, study was a refreshing change from what I had been doing – for them, in most cases, it was not. And, unlike students who remained on campus or amongst the student fraternity in the evenings and at weekends, I came home to a complete and enforced change – cooking tea, preparing lunch boxes for the next day, washing, ironing, etc., and generally caring for my children's needs. A necessary break for the brain. When we did eventually settle to homework it became a true family occasion, with me joining in!

My contemporaries, particularly in Linguistics, included other mature students also - some already speech therapists, or training for similar careers. Some students were in their mid- to late 20s, having messed up at school and had come to see the importance of education later in life. The one disappointment of our mature years, or at least for myself with children, is that I missed out on the opportunities in the pubs, student digs, or other hang-outs, for debates and discussions on assignments, etc. Occasionally, the more mature of us would have brief encounters in the coffee shop after lectures, but overall, my assignments, at least, did not benefit from broader input.

Divergent Pathways

I was completely comfortable with the path I had chosen, even though it involved hard work studying as well as managing the family. My first Christmas holiday was to be spent with my youngest, unmarried, sister as it was the children's turn to spend the time with their Father at his parents' home in Worthing. This gave me an opportunity to catch up on some reading.

My sister had recently joined an evangelical church with quite fundamental views. Little did I realise that this combination of academia and religion was to cause problems. I was castigated for my reading matter, for it was not 'solely of God'. I tried to explain my reasons for undertaking a degree, but my sister was not to be appeased. I explained that, having spent some years working for the Church, I felt I was now being led to learn more of the world God had created, and that my work in the future was to be 'in the world'. When she claimed that we, as Catholics, were not even Christians because we were not baptised by full immersion, she managed to upset the rest of the family too. No amount of explanation would change her view, so we spent most of Christmas in separate rooms; I, in order to be able to catch up on my necessary university reading without causing too much offence to my hostess.

When I got home, I wrote her a detailed explanation of my spiritual history which I believe she may not have been fully aware of at the time. I told her I was convinced that this was the path down which God, for whatever reason, was leading me. Some months later she confessed that she had been a 'baby Christian' at the time, and peace was eventually restored, and within the family too.

Squash

Term time began again. After leaving school I had always harboured dreams of playing squash, but never had the opportunity. With a dodgy spine, I suppose I would have been a bit nervous even had the opportunity arisen. My skiing holiday in Arosa at aged 17 had ended almost disastrously when, after skiing every day for a week, there was a national holiday for New Year's Day when no lessons occurred. (On Christmas Day, everything continued as normal). We went off for a walk instead. My back was beginning to feel rather uncomfortable when I suddenly slipped and fell, and, because of the pain, I could barely heave myself out of the way of an oncoming, horse-drawn sleigh that was speeding down the hill. I ended up spending the remaining week of the holiday in bed on my back, which at the time was diagnosed as a slipped disc.

I had done no sport except for walking, and a little local cycling to and from the shops, since I got married and had the children – there had been no time or opportunity. So, when asked by one of my fellow students if I would like to play squash at the facilities at the University, my new-found confidence and enthusiasm found me saying "Yes!". I found that I could play quite a good game without moving much around the court as I had quite powerful shoulders - we were, after all, both beginners. It was an exhilarating game but I soon found I had to give it up because, though it was a great boost to my morale to be able to play, my spine was not quite so happy, even using my relatively stationery position on the court.

DISASTER

Disaster strikes ...

My euphoric bubble was soon to burst. In my second year at University, I reached the summer holidays only to discover that the Department of Social Security had made some sort of error in allowing me travel and childcare expenses during term time. They deemed, therefore, that I was only entitled to £15 per week for the fifteen-week duration of this second summer University vacation. Somehow, they were expecting me to make my three-termly study grants last for the whole twelve months.

Single-parent mature students were still a novelty in the early '80s, the UEA being a forerunner in accepting them, and their needs were not considered in the Government's further education policy of the time. However hard I fought, this fact was simply emphasised. I even wrote to the Parliamentary Department concerned, the head of which was the person destined to become the future Prime Minister, John Major. The response was a typical three-page Government reply that said nothing very much and was certainly not going to help me at the time.

I was getting no maintenance for the children or for myself so, for the next step, I was advised to take Court proceedings in an attempt to rectify this. Such action was certainly not going to help the immediate situation as the formalities involved meant, even if successful (which was doubtful), I would not have money in time to tide us over the summer. The only solution that came to mind was to sell the bungalow.

Trying to sell the family home during the final year of studies was something I knew I could not cope with, notwithstanding managing the three children and the home-keeping - burdensome-enough tasks in themselves. I got so behind with my essays because the stress had caused such a tight band around my forehead, that study became impossible. I went to discuss the situation with my Tutor who suggested I could take a year's sabbatical and resume the studies the following year once I had sorted things out. Meanwhile he offered me a few days leave to think about things and suggested I ask my other lecturers for extensions to the deadlines of my outstanding essays.

... But not for long

The very fact I had this option was a weight lifted from my shoulders. With a clearer head, I had eureka moment regarding our financial crisis – I had a student bank account. I would go to the Bank and ask if I could have an overdraft to tide me over until the end of my course, and I would then sell the home to repay the money.

After the break, having sorted out the overdraft with the Bank, I decided that to continue with the university course would be the best option. To have to undergo the complications of re-negotiating with the DSS, and maybe losing the impetus of studying after a year out, missing out on keeping up with the friends I had made, etc., my degree might never happen. So, roof intact for the time being at least, and the children able to remain settled in their current schools (for who knows where we might have ended up in social housing?) I finished the summer term of 1986 and set my sights on my final year.

This made me think about my 'eureka' moments. Surely this was the Holy Spirit in action? My mind was too busy, and maybe too confused at the time, to recognise His working in my life.

Counselling

Then came a second blow. One of my friends happened to be secretary to the head of the Counselling Department, Brian Thorne. I originally got to know her through the Samaritans where she was one of the leaders. Occasionally, we would meet up for lunch in between my lectures and we would catch up on the counselling world, among other things.

When Christine realised where my degree was supposed to be leading me, she placed something of a dampener on my ambitions. She told me that the local area was saturated with good counsellors. This was because of the exceptional Counselling Department at the UEA which not only saw to student (and staff) needs, but also gave training courses for those interested in the world of counselling which I occasionally took part in when my responsibilities allowed. Consequently, there were very many very good counsellors in the

Norwich area. It was becoming world-renowned because of Brian who was gaining international notoriety because his writing and lectures. He was also to become the first Professor of Counselling in the country.

Even a very good registered counsellor should only work a limited number of hours per week because of the stress of the job; the deep nature of some of the problems presented, and the effort of trying not to take on board the problems of your counselees. It could, at best, be considered a part-time job and, although quite well paid, the income generated would be insufficient to support three children, myself and the mortgage. Something of a rethink was required.

Meanwhile, my course on the Philosophy of Religion was becoming imminent. My disturbed feelings about God seem to bother me more and more as the course approached. Would I (I naively thought) find all the answers regarding God? Would the course help my seemingly damaged relationship with Him? I could not quite put my finger on what was bothering me about it.

Brian

I happened to mention this to my friend Christine, Brian's Secretary, at one of our lunchtime meetings. She suggested I had some counselling sessions with Brian. I protested that I didn't feel in need of counselling; my issues weren't that disturbing. "Well, it wouldn't do any harm. He's a very spiritual person. I'm sure he could help." I protested again that surely he would be too busy with those in more desperate need of his help.

The standard six sessions I had with Brian were amazing - he managed to turn most of my distorted thinking around by the end. When I mentioned, among other things, that I felt God had abandoned me over the past six or so years, he took me aback somewhat with his reply, indicating that St Teresa of Avila (my most

61

admired female saint and whose name I had adopted for Confirmation) had felt abandoned by God for many more years than that, so why should I be worried? This thought that I was in the company of the saints - or a saint at least - with my feelings, made me feel a little better, but was not hugely helpful at the time. Years later, I remembered these words when I came across her autobiography, 'St Teresa of Avila by herself'. Reading this book had a very profound effect on my heart and my relationship with God became fully restored. God's ways are, indeed, mysterious.

In later years, I came to realise that, quite often when we attempt to evangelise and our words seem to fall on stony ground, we don't know that we haven't sown a seed that may sprout and fruit months, or even years, later.

THE GAP MONTHS

Graduation

I never aspired to a First, but a 2/1 would have pleased me more than the 2/2 I achieved. After Graduation, attended by my parents and Philip, my Samaritan mentor and University sponsor, I spent the summer looking for jobs. As the children were still young, one still being at primary level, it had to be part-time. The counselling door was pretty much closed so I had to think of another way of generating enough income to support our needs as a family, and ease us out of this benefit trap. In which direction to head was far from clear.

Another door opened when a friend, who was on the Norwich School PTA, heard of a vacancy in the School. It was as Assistant Librarian, starting in September. This was ideal as it was during school hours and would give me the school holidays free to be with the children. It would work as a stopgap. It was not the most brain-stretching of jobs, cataloguing and stacking books, etc., but I also had the task of supervising Fifth- and Sixth- formers who came in as a class for their study periods. That was far more of a challenge! In between, however, there was plenty of time to think in which direction my serious career move should be.

Education or Hesitation?

During my early days in the Norwich School library, I suddenly had an inspiration that I should further my education by enrolling for a business diploma course at City College. What pushed me into this I am never quite certain. Where do such promptings come from? I supposed that managerial or administrative skills would be necessary if I was going to earn sufficient money to shake off the social benefit mantle, whether in employment or running my own business. It was a two-year course involving only Thursday evenings. As I jauntily rolled up for my first evening, I felt this irrational notion that my Grandfather, who had been eminently successful in business during his lifetime, was behind me, urging me on, convincing me it was the right thing to be doing. At the time, I had no idea where it was going to lead...

I suppose I was hedging all my bets - the two-year course was a way to maximise my options as I was still unable to work full-time because my children were still dependent, the youngest, by then, being only eleven. Working full-time as a single parent with three children, one not even in her teens, did not seem a sensible option. The business qualification could be a valuable passport to some managerial post later.

Talents

Good fortune continued to follow me. I had become friends with a solicitor with his own group of practices whom I met at a party. He was a very philanthropic person and I would prefer not to think that he saw me as a needy case, but having him as a close friend was a great boost to my morale. We would occasionally have supper together and it was on one such occasion when I discussed with him my future career problems, and a few of my ideas for possibilities for the way ahead.

Among some of these ideas, my thoughts regarding running my own business must have cropped up. I had long held what I had considered to be an irrational urge to run a small business, or at least to take some sort of active role in one. I had never considered it a true possibility as I was always terribly lacking in confidence and had no direct experience – or experience that could be counted as positive. I presumed this dream was due to some gene lurking in my system inherited from my Grandfathers. My paternal Grandfather, and his Father before him, my Great-Grandfather, had both been eminently successful businessmen in their day. The latter had started a lace manufacturing business just before the First World War in 1912, and the former built it up to become the largest manufacturer of lace trimmings in the world during the early part of the 20th century.

My poor level of confidence, and lack of any money, had never made running a business a realistic option. I presumed, too, this ambition, if it was ever to be realised, was destined to come to fruition only alongside a husband who was bringing in a sensible level of household income. In other words, it would appear I had in mind nothing more than a glorified hobby or 'cottage industry'. I expect that this was so that the outright success of a small business was not so important (my lack of confidence again!). Now I was in a new situation. What other options did I have?

Handicaps and hindrances

Circumstances had changed. My confidence had improved dramatically as a result of my three years at university, and now there was a pressing need to earn beyond what could be achieved through a cottage industry. The possibility of failure, however, was not now an option.

My thoughts initially were for a tool hire business. I had had a certain amount of experience in this field with my (ex-) husband whose expertise was in the manufacturing of furniture and joinery. He was a very practical person who also used different machinery from time-to-time for his DIY activities at home. I could think of nothing else I could do, but there were problems. I had a spinal incapacity that had caused me difficulties since the age of 15. Lifting and overdoing things did not suit it, but then I could hire staff to do any shifting that was required.

Usually a small business succeeds because the owner puts in near 24/7 hours in a sole capacity, doing most of the jobs themselves to minimise costs - at least initially. With this type of business, for me, this would not be possible – I would require physical help, and I had the children to consider. I would be even more reliant on staff if my spine ran into difficulties and it became necessary for me to have a few days off. Could a new small business sustain such overheads?

The Philanthropist

My legal friend came up with a stunning proposal - he suggested backing me financially! His suggestion was that I should set up in estate agency. Because of new legislation in the mid-1980's, legal firms, building societies and insurance companies were buying out estate agencies to expand their businesses.

Did I want to be under someone's patronage? Did I want high profile street premises? I felt sure his suggestion would not be coming without strings attached. Not to succeed would not be an option, particularly as I had no wish to lose another person's friendship or their money, however much they might be able to afford it. I had no experience of the estate agency industry. I said I would think about it.

The Conception

That evening, as the thoughts mulled over in my mind, I prayed for guidance as is my wont when difficult decisions must be made. Here was someone who was prepared to offer me a major role in running a business - even without initial experience in the field. I was quite elated at the thought that this person had such an amount of confidence in my abilities - a further morale booster! But did I want to be beholden, financially or otherwise?

Estate agency appealed as a career as I loved people and I loved houses. My Father would frequently take us for walks around our locality which contained some quite large and varied late-Victorian houses. He would often stop to admire special features - for what purpose I never did quite divine other than an assumption that he simply had a passion for properties and their architecture. I must have inherited this gene from my Father, alongside my Grandfathers' genes for entrepreneurship.

Then a more interesting prospect materialised. I could manage and let properties instead of becoming an agent for the buying and selling of them, and for this I could equally gain experience. The advantage was that I would not necessarily need high street premises, therefore the funding required would be minimal in comparison. I could even start off by managing a few properties from home to see how it panned out. If successful, I could carry on; if not, then a handful of properties to manage alongside a full-time job would hopefully generate the sort of income I needed to achieve my ambition of leaving social dependence behind. But my confidence was still not as assured as I had thought.

I found a part-time job for two evenings a week and Saturday afternoons, working in an estate agent's office, which fitted in with my other responsibilities. The company was Bush & Spelman in King Street, Norwich. I am still in touch with the very bubbly, half-Spanish senior girl whom I shadowed – a brilliant mentor. I filled in for her during the unsocial hours the agency remained open. I had time to get the children their tea before leaving Michelle in charge, with our neighbour, Mabel, in the adjoining bungalow to oversee any problems, and I was back before their bedtimes. There was a lettings department at Bush & Spelman's, but their work was carried out upstairs so, unfortunately, I had no contact of any note with them.

A MAN'S WORLD

DMS

Meanwhile, the Diploma in Management Studies course was absorbing a deal of my attention also. There were two other females on the course beside myself, and initially we made up less than 10% of the class. The idea of women in business was still in its infancy. We were made very welcome by the course tutor, but it was not long before discrimination against females entered the class environment, mainly from the tutor himself. Looking back, it may well have been to see how tough we were - to see if we had the metal to stay the course. One girl dropped out before the end of the first year.

Most of the students were already in managerial positions and had been sent by their firms for their, and ultimately their firms', betterment. This was one of the criteria for admission to the course. The second was a university degree – I seemed to be the only student that had been accepted on this ground alone, which put me at a slight disadvantage as the teaching was geared towards enhancing the individual's ability in his (or her) workplace role. Michelle, my remaining fellow female student, and I, quietly endured the ribbing which emanated principally from the tutor, and we both survived the two years.

Weaknesses

In class, if we didn't understand something, Michelle and I were always ready to ask the questions – the men were too afraid to lose face. This I learnt from the young Assistant Manager of the UEA Sports Centre with whom I had become friends. We often did our homework together. My big weakness was statistics, and I was convinced that my inability to fully grasp these concepts would mean I would fail in the subject. My young friend seemed to know the male and female psyche well and he assured me that this would not be the case. He said he was convinced that some of the chaps on the course were equally at sea with some of the subjects but were too macho to raise their hands to ask questions when they didn't understand. Sure enough, we girls both gained our diplomas and three of the 27 men failed.

For the second year, we were told we would need to complete a project that would enhance our work situation and benefit the company for which we worked. I was working a few hours per week for the estate agency. The agency had not sent me on this course and I was working there as a part-time assistant learning the ropes. As a mere part-timer, I didn't think they would appreciate my audacity if I suddenly started involving them in a project that would purportedly improve their business, and my standing in it – particularly as I wasn't planning to stay.

Statistics

My neighbour back home was a great support and encourager. Mabel, our babysitter-cum-third Granny who had lived there previously, had sadly died the previous year and the bungalow was now occupied by a female top-level medic named Ann. Presumably, having highly achieved in her own profession, she was eager to see others of her gender pushing their abilities in the male-dominated world of work as it still was in the late 'eighties.

Ann and I had had many chats over the eighteen months since the proposal from my solicitor-friend was first put to me. She began regularly questioning me about my thoughts on running a business. When WAS I going to get it started? She was getting quite impatient with me, so again I took this as a compliment and was encouraged because she must have thought I was on to a good thing. This triggered some thoughts regarding my college project. I could research the viability of setting up a letting agency. That would still not commit me to doing so. If the research proved negative, then I would be let off the hook. Did I truly have the guts to run a business anyway?

Little did I foresee that the project I had decided on would rely heavily on statistics – the subject at which I was least able. I had arrived at the conclusion that I had some form of numerate dyslexia, especially when it came to the type of logic involved in the sphere of numbers and statistics. When at University I had also struggled with elements such as Venn diagrams, etc. and my Logics Tutor described me as having a 'reverse logic'. Unfortunately, he could not define exactly what having a reverse logic meant.

For me, when it came to logic and numbers, I seemed to get things the wrong way around. My logic in other respects has been described as very good when it comes to analysing situations not involving numbers. Now I had chosen to embark on this project which relied heavily on statistics. It seemed there was no other way forward by which I could produce a thesis to satisfy the course requirement, especially as I did not have the alternative option of a serious employment role on which to base such a project.

The Diploma

The Norfolk County Council had brought out a twelve-year structure plan for the period 1988-2001 which was a great help. I soon discovered that the way statistics are presented can be manipulated to suit one's purpose. However, as I had a serious interest in the outcome, I had to make sure that what I was providing was the truth regarding the viability of properties that were likely to be available for rent, and how I would fare amongst the opposition.

Much to my surprise I achieved an 'A-' for my thesis with the comment: "This is excellent work ... The minus sign in my grading simply reflects my own inability to regard anything as perfect." It was a great accolade from the one who had tried his utmost to scare the ladies off the course by his constant gibes bordering on discrimination, and from one who was aware of my difficulties grasping statistics. Michelle and I had stuck it out to the end and we had both passed, allowing us to add 'DMS' (Diploma in Management Studies) to our title where appropriate. (As already mentioned, three of the men failed).

The most important outcome of my project, notwithstanding the mark it achieved? My research revealed there was plenty of room for another letting agency - particularly a specialist agency, as there were none available in the immediate vicinity.

~

REFLECTION:

COMFORT ZONES

How does one transform one's character and, potentially, one's path in life? Does it help to have those about you who can be open and honest with you?

When the rich man came to Jesus and asked what should he do to inherit eternal life, Jesus was frank with him and told him, among other things, that he should sell everything and give to the poor to be assured of gaining treasure in heaven. Although the rich man was largely following the ten commandments, he had one personality trait that he was not prepared to alter – his fondness for his riches, his possessions (Luke 18:20-23). Did he lose out? He no doubt carried on with his good life but missed out on the benefits that an even deeper commitment could have brought him because he lacked the courage to make the changes.

Every now and then we must step out of our comfort zone to achieve an ultimate gain. I had people around me, encouraging me to take the further steps towards becoming self-sufficient – my Samaritan mentor, my neighbour, my philanthropic friend – all had the confidence that I could do it, but I lacked it. I could have remained in my relative comfort zone and continue to survive, supported financially by State handouts. After much persistence from those around me, my mind was eventually turned and I threw lack of courage and confidence - and caution, to the wind…. Then I was able to achieve what I had never dreamt was possible.

THOUGHTS FOR DISCUSSION

1. Sometimes we wrap our traits around us like a cosy blanket. It is hard to step out into the cold unknown and change our habits of a lifetime. What would help you do this?

2. When life seems in a bit of a muddle it sometimes takes another to view things dispassionately and make suggestions. How open would you be to the advice of others?

3. Do you have people around you who need encouragement? Are you confident about being honest with them?

--ooOoo--

Chapter 5

SETTING UP

GETTING STARTED

Location

We lived in Brundall, on the fringe of the Norfolk Broads - a beautiful wetland area and a haven for wildlife. Historically, the Broads are man-made peat diggings in low-lying land that spans the area between Norwich and the coast. As much of the area is below sea level, these peat-diggings have become flooded over time, thereby attracting much wildlife and migratory birds. They are linked by rivers and cuts that have caused the area to develop into a major tourist attraction for sailing and family cruising.

As I write, discussions are under way to designate the area unofficially as a National Park. The largest part of the area is governed by Broadland District Council. When we first moved to the area the Council was still known as the District of Blofield and Flegg. Historically, Blofield was a major rural community, having its own courthouse and mail sorting office. Today it is a mere village that has been superseded in importance and popularity by neighbouring Brundall because of its river and rail access. The development of housing in the '50s and '60s led to Blofield and Brundall becoming conjoined. Eventually the local Blofield and Flegg Council morphed under the new title, Broadland District Council.

When we first arrived in Norfolk in 1973, with our toddler daughter, Michelle, and nine-week-old son, Paul, I could not help but feel it was pretty much a flat, barren land devoid of interest. No hills or mountains, no pretty villages such as in Derbyshire, the stomping ground of my youth, or Sussex or Wales where we had previously lived. It seemed just a mass of sprawling marshland, spattered with a few cows and sheep, windmills in various states of disrepair, and the odd distant farm. Even the villages seemed dull, consisting of one main road, nearly always named "The Street", with terraced houses or farm workers' dwellings which resembled the rather bland council houses of the Midlands, and maybe a single shop-cum-Post Office, and a pub or two. Occasionally there would be large gates, with hedges or fences either side, enclosing driveways to some mysterious, invisible, large dwelling behind. People either love Norfolk or they hate it.

Hidden Gems

After a few Sundays with an OS map aiding us in the discovery of otherwise hidden tracks, we found walks that took us to Broads and rivers, alive with nature and peace, that lay tucked away from the hustle and bustle of everyday life. As a Midlander by birth, the species of birds, flora and fauna discovered were a rarity and a joy to the heart. I began to love the area with its mystery of whatever life lay around the next turn – its quiet, hidden waterways, the wildlife in winter reasserting its hold on its native territory after the intrusive holiday makers have vanished, and the windy North Sea lapping along its expansive sandy beaches. Norfolk's gems mainly lie hidden from modern modes of transport (Modern? As I write it is 2015 and Norfolk does not sport even one single piece of motorway – the main route to London, the A11, having only just had its final stretch of dualling completed!). One needs a boat, a bike or strong legs to appreciate Norfolk's delights.

Company title & Logo

It was 1988, midway through my final year of the DMS course, when I began to seriously put my mind to setting up a letting agency. As herons were birds that frequent the Broads 'Heron' seemed a good name to adopt as a company identifier - emblematic of the area in which I expected to be operating. Only afterwards did someone remind me that herons were thieving birds, often seen standing at the edge of garden ponds waiting to pounce on some unsuspecting fish. Not exactly the image I wanted to create, and certainly not the style of business I wished to adopt! By the time I learnt this fact, unfortunately it was too late to change the name. I was not native to the area myself, and fortunately many of my clients-to-be were also from other parts of the country - referred to by the 'Nor' (th) folk as "furriners" (foreigners) in the local dialect - so they, too, were largely ignorant of this ornithological fact.

Having chosen the name 'Heron', I needed a logo. It began as a slightly bulbous 'H'. We then placed a giant circumflex accent over the top to represent a roof. The roof then acquired a chimney and it was subsequently decided the 'H' should become straightened back to its more natural state to represent the walls of a house. We then transformed it again to become a highlighted 3D 'H'. For a while this seemed sufficient until, as a final inspiration, a heron was added, threaded through the middle of the 'H'.

As I wanted to offer a specialist service caring for peoples' homes rather than property purchased purely for investment, I added 'Homecare' to the title and we became 'Heron Homecare'. Care homes for the elderly in the 1980s were still a relatively new concept. It was some years later when I realised there was such a care home in an obscure lane on the edge of the village known as 'Heronlea'. We had begun to receive misplaced phone calls asking if it was convenient to visit Mr so-and-so; or, "What time is Mrs P......'s funeral this afternoon?" With the advent of a near exponential increase in the senior population of the country, so did the number of care homes increase in the early '90s. I finally decided we needed a name-change and the more conventional title of Heron Property Management was introduced in 1996.

The First Property

My neighbour, Ann, a single lady who had highly achieved in her own career, was still on my back about getting my business started, obviously realising I was on to a good thing. She could not understand my hesitation. My youngest child, Lizzy, was now at Secondary School and all three children were becoming reasonably independent. Ann had offered me the loan of her computer, but, being the perfectionist that I am, I was still acquiring knowledge of how to carry off the whole enterprise.

Ann returned from a party one weekend and told me she had met Lady S….. During the party patter it transpired she had a son who was an airline pilot with Cathay Pacific based in Hong Kong where he was living with his family. He had just bought a property in Brundall as a base to be near his mother when he visited the UK. He was looking for someone to manage the property for him in his absence. Ann had told her about me and she arrived back from the party with a name and address. This son of Lady S….. was only in the country for the next ten days, living in the property he had just purchased.

Now or Never

With my neighbour's intervention, it was now or never… I hastily cobbled together an application form with all the questions I thought would be relevant, and very timorously I went the half mile down the road and knocked on the door. I was sure that my ham-fisted attempt at an application form, and, in retrospect, no assenting documents for the prospective landlords to sign, would at least warrant an "We'll think about it", meaning they would be interviewing more competent and experienced agencies before deciding to which one they would entrust their valuable asset. The chances of it being me seemed exceedingly remote.

My feigned confidence and apparent knowledge earned me the business - much to my surprise. I had gained my first property, a modern three bedroomed detached house, in a very desirable village! It seemed the months of preparation had stood me in good stead.

COMPLETING THE SET UP

Initial Investment

I was now bulldozed into completing the set-up for my business. It was not too difficult to create headed notepaper on the loaned computer as a temporary measure until I could afford to have proper notepaper printed. My initial investment for starting the business came out of my own pocket (as opposed to being borrowed). It was the princely sum of £15 (this was 1989) for the cost of placing an advert in the local Eastern Daily Press for tenants for this first property. This was the only outlay from my own pocket.

My legal friend who had offered to back me, seemed not to mind that I had turned down his offer of financial assistance. Now, of course, I could manage without it as I was operating from home, and on borrowed equipment. Instead, his philanthropy extended to helping me with legal advice and an offer to provide the tenancy agreements for which he made no charge. I was blessed indeed!

Area Covered

With a compass and a wall map I had traced a radius of 25 miles from Brundall as the area I would cover. This seemed a reasonable maximum distance for inspecting properties without travel costs eating too much into the profits. This covered Norwich city as well as the Broadland area. Norfolk covers an area of 5,371 km² (approx. 3338 square miles) and, compared to the rest of England, is relatively sparsely populated. As the business eventually came to be in such demand, the radius was extended by a further five miles, then by another five, so that very soon we were covering most of Norfolk and north Suffolk.

Forward Planning

I worked out a plan that if I could achieve one new property per month during the first eight months then I would know the business was viable. This would bring me to September when the children would be moving up a year in their schools and if I did not achieve that target I would have to find another job. I could then manage, during my spare time, the handful of properties I would have hopefully gained to date, as top-up income. I was still working at the estate agency two evenings in the week, and on Saturday afternoons, to boost the coffers, and Social Security topped up the difference.

I continued reading up on letting law and anything to do with running a small business, especially anything biased towards lettings. Broadland District Council, the Banks, and the local press office - Eastern Counties Newspapers, were all very keen to promote small businesses and I attended several of their free courses, some of which were designed specifically to encourage women into business.

Doing Different

The research for my DMS project had thrown up the fact that there were a handful of letting agents in Norwich that dealt mainly with flats and bedsits within Norwich – mostly properties that had been bought by their owners purely as investment. There was a notable absence of anyone dealing with the more rural properties, and nobody had aimed directly at the larger properties, these being mostly their owner's homes into which they had plans to return at some time in the future.

I decided that one three- or four-bedroomed house would provide the income of two, three, or even four flats or bedsits. The additional bonus to managing larger houses was that they were more likely to attract established families and I would be dealing with one set of tenants producing a fairly guaranteed income, whereas the equivalent income obtainable from three or four flats or bedsits would likely provide 3-5 times the hassle and an uncertain income. The larger properties were also likely to attract tenants who had probably owned and looked after their own places and were, therefore, more likely to have knowledge of how to care for them properly.

Working from home I would have few overheads and, therefore, could spend more time on a caring service for people who wanted to let out their personal homes rather than properties bought purely as investment. Because of my physical state (I had a recurring, and seemingly worsening, yet not fully diagnosed, spinal condition), the less aggravation I had to cope with meant more energy to be better able to provide this caring service which was my principal aim. More money for less energy expended seemed a good maxim.

UP AND RUNNING

Clash of Interest

One of the first problems I encountered was my part-time employment with Bush & Spelman. What I was doing was effectively beginning a business that clashed in interest with their lettings department. I needed the additional income this employment afforded until I could guarantee I was on the way to success with my own venture. My conscience got the better of me and I decided to own up to what I was about. I would have to do battle with the Benefits Office regarding the difference this loss of income would entail and trust they would make up the difference.

It seems the God of surprises was around every corner. When I approached the boss to tender my notice and explained why, I was informed there were changes afoot. One of the building societies was buying out the estate agency arm of the business (for which I was directly working) and David Bush was planning to carry on his lettings department independently. I would, therefore, not be a threat to the business if I remained. Blessings for my business seemed to abound and confirm my way forward.

Norwich Terraces

Among my first properties was a smart, mid-size, early 19th Century terrace in the centre of Norwich, the style of which, as a company, we came to refer to as a two-and-a-half bedroomed property – the design quite popular of the era where the third bedroom - a very small room - had to be accessed via the second bedroom. These properties normally had hall entrances, whereas with smaller terraces the front door opened directly into the living room. Originally, all had outbuildings housing the one and only toilet, but by the early twentieth century most terraces had bathroom extensions built either above the extended kitchen, or beyond, on the ground floor, with an additional back hallway in between. There were, of course, larger terraces linked for convenience of space in the fast-growing city centres.

The Second Overseas Landlord

I usually met all my landlords personally at the properties I was asked to take on. There is always an exception. The landlord to this, my first, mid-size terrace was living in Canada - a friend of a friend. I viewed the property courtesy of a key given to me by my friend to whom it had been entrusted, and the negotiations with the landlord were done over the phone. He twice visited my office on his return to the UK but on each occasion I was out on the road. I understood he was tall, with light-coloured hair, and handsome.

The Sack

Whilst the children were still young, among other part-time jobs, I had done some office work at a local plant nursery at Witton, a neighbouring village. I worked in the site office for a few hours, three times per week, doing the bookkeeping. The owner's home was a bungalow which nestled behind a thick conifer hedge on the northern perimeter of the nursery. The owner, Geoff, a fairly elderly man, would often complain about his younger wife, saying that she was always spying on him from behind the conifers, and sometimes even threatened him with a pitchfork. I took his words with a bit of a pinch of salt. I do believe she was something of a tyrant, though, as the nursery staff referred to her as "'Er Indoors".

One day, after I had been there some weeks, Geoff came up to me and said "I am going to have to part company with you. 'Er Indoors' is making my life such a misery – she thinks I'm having an affair with you." I had to laugh. In broad daylight, with staff milling in and out of the shed all day?! But he was serious. I got dismissed for being the 'other woman'.

Royal Air Force

Some years later, it turned out that Geoff had become divorced, had sold the business, and had moved into a smart house in Blofield. When I met up with him again, he was in the throes of selling this Blofield property and invited me to his house-leaving party - not just for old-times' sake, but he had heard about my business and he wanted me to meet someone he thought would be of interest to me.

This person was a representative from the Royal Air Force who was overseeing a new scheme adopted by the RAF whereby their personnel were being encouraged to purchase property as an investment for their future when they left the Force. This guy was buying property on their behalf, and he was looking for an agent to manage their Norfolk-based ones - this being one of the areas with the largest property price increases at that time. I became that agent, and Geoffrey's home, which was being bought for an Air Commodore, was to be the first of many such properties filling my portfolio.

Confidence Boosters

Two further incidents occurred after only six months of trading which enhanced my confidence enormously. One morning I answered the phone to a senior London-based executive of a well-known stock market-listed company. He wanted to invest in property in Norfolk as he had heard it was the up-and-coming area where property was still cheap – which was the case in the late 'eighties. I was still somewhat in awe of these high-flying executives.

The properties I would normally recommend would be a city- or suburb-based two bedroomed type. There is by far and away the greatest demand for these properties, therefore rents, pro rata, tend to be higher with the consequence of a more profitable return on investment. The reason for this demand is that renters tend to be mainly single people or young 'starter' couples. They often want a spare room to use as an office/guest room. With no children, and in the case of couples, two incomes, this category is where rent is more easily afforded. The market forces of supply and demand kick in. Once a prospective tenant has a family in tow, quite likely a three-plus bedroomed property would be required. With the drain on income of dependants, and often only one earner - or at best an additional part-time earner, available income for rent is more limited, therefore the percentage of rent pro rata to the landlord's investment tends to be more restrained.

I asked this executive, with what confidence I could muster, what type of property he was after and what price bracket was he interested in? "I was hoping you would advise me. After all, you are the expert" was his reply. Obviously, price was no object. His latter phrase, however, had me mulling over this point for some time after. Yes, he might be top-dog in his company, in his sphere of interest and training, but there were probably many areas in his life, besides the whys and where-fors of purchasing property, about which he had little or no idea. And, yes, I had done research and, despite my meagre few months of running a lettings agency, I had to acknowledge that, regardless of this latter fact, I had far more experience in this field than he!

From Maisonettes to Mansions

Another morning call, by coincidence - and around the time of my early foray into running my business – was from a prospective landlord who had been abandoned by his wife in a 13-bedroomed mansion in Tasburgh, in south Norfolk. He felt the property was far too big for just him and he was thinking of letting it. Was this the sort of thing I dealt with? Having set myself up to cater for the more up-market properties, I gritted my teeth and said "Yes, of course"!

We duly arranged an appointment for me to view the property. As I drove up the long drive with acres of garden to boot, I began to consider my folly. Would I be able to find tenants for this size of property? How would I carry out the detailing of the inventory with, no doubt, some valuable paintings and other assets that may be left, the definition of which would be totally beyond my knowledge? I would not begin to know how to describe some of the historic artefacts that were likely to adorn the place. I could not lose face by displaying my ignorance, and at that point I began to think of turning around and abandoning the appointment - but then I would equally lose face. I began to regret my boldness. "Dear God, what have I done?"

'Dear God' answered me. As I was welcomed by the landlord and ushered in, ideas began pouring into my head. Finding tenants would be a gamble as no doubt the prospective landlord would be aware. With regard to the inventory (and there were some rather grand portraits and other artefacts in the main hall alone!), with the monthly commission achievable from the rent I could obtain for such a place, I could afford to engage a professional inventory company. No doubt the owner would also be contacting other agents for comparison - I might (hopefully?) not even get the business.

To my surprise, I was commissioned to manage the property and I did find tenants for it – a commercial company that wished to establish a foothold in Norfolk. In the end, I believe there was some complication with the landlord's insurance or mortgage because, at a relatively late stage, he pulled the property from us and decided to sell. Nonetheless, I felt the experience was a feather in my cap and another boost to my confidence.

The exercise was not entirely a waste of time, which was not an infrequent occurrence in this type of business anyway. Once he sold his mansion, this prospective landlord became one of my tenants as he wished to move into something smaller. We found him one of our 'normal' relatively large properties and eased his comfort.

The Delights...

I couldn't believe my good fortune. I had a job which enabled me to drive around the beautiful Norfolk countryside, and often up to the coast, and I was earning my living doing so. Coastal visits I would try and arrange around the middle of the day so that I could have my lunch break taking a walk on the beach, and/or (especially if raining) eating our wonderful fish and chips in the car overlooking the sea. If I had inspections or visits in or around Norwich, then my lunch hour would be taken up undertaking the family shopping.

I was very strict with my office hours, particularly necessary when working from home. I was in my 'office' from 9.00am until 5.30pm, with an hour for lunch. It was wonderful to feel one was in control of one's own time, particularly being able, when necessary, to take a break from the discipline of the routine when an occasion arose - for example when there were specific needs of the children, such as sports days or medical appointments, and even for my own essential needs.

At the end of the working day it was straight into the kitchen to prepare a meal for myself and the children. This created a necessary, and complete break between the routines of 'office' and home. It did not prevent me, out of choice, from returning later in the evening, when all was peaceful and quiet, to complete some paperwork or accounting, or to make a phone call to an overseas landlord living in a different time zone.

…and Downsides

On the negative side, society was still unused to females holding managerial positions, let alone running their own businesses. Some chauvinist males perhaps looked on me as a bit of a joke, despite entrusting their properties to my care. More than once a landlord would turn up on my doorstep at some unreasonable hour, maybe just as I was ushering the children to be ready for the school run - well before the 9am general office-opening hours.

Even my very pleasant landlord from Hong Kong arrived one morning at 7am, jet-lagged and just off his 'plane. He had time to kill, so he said, and thought he would pay me a visit to see how things were going. I had no option but to update him on his investment in my dressing gown – not my favourite way of conducting business! This was the downside to working from what, to an outsider, would appear as an informal office in my home. Or maybe I was 'too kind' and they treated me more as a friend than a person to whom they had entrusted their property – but then even friends do not usually arrive on your doorstep at seven in the morning!

On another occasion, my visiting daughter and family were all loaded in the car ready to go off to some Boxing Day event when a car drew up blocking our exit. It was a tenant who had lost his keys, (I think he must have been out all night celebrating) so I had little option but to halt proceedings, open the office, collect the key to the key safe and extract from the safe the spare key to the property he was renting. Then I had to get him to sign for it before he, and we, could continue our day's planned mission – he quite probably to his bed to overcome his hangover.

PROBLEMS & PROGRESS

Cramped Conditions

He who was guiding my destiny did not let up. My first twelve properties had been managed from a shelf set up in my bedroom, and the foot of my bed doubled as an office chair during the day.

By 1990 the business had migrated from my bedroom and was now being run from the very small dining area of our home. It was not the most convenient place with a young family who had to pass through to get to the only living area (our meals were eaten in the kitchen). This became an aggravation, particularly during school holidays, and not just for the children but for the business too. However, the plus side for the children, with me working from home, was that at least I was around for general supervision and when their needs were more specific. Being my own boss I could also make a judgement about when to spend more focussed time with them – especially once I began employing staff.

The bungalow was by no means big. Not only was space a problem for the family, and even more so for the business, but another downside was access to the property. The only way for clients to reach us was along a footpath accessed either end by residential cul-de-sacs, so parking was also an issue. Another problem for my desired professional image was that the building was a linked bungalow in the middle of a housing estate. Ideally, I needed to move to somewhere more accessible and practical, but I simply could not afford to do so.

A Hiccup

By a strange quirk of fate, I encountered a seemingly negative situation that was to prove an interim solution to the problem of office space. Was this the good Lord's hand at work again?

In 1990, fortune took an unusual turn of events. The family lace manufacturing company had its share value re-assessed by the Inland Revenue. I owned a handful of these shares, a legacy from my Grandfather. These had been augmented subsequently by my Father who had given some of his shares to me and my siblings as a means of off-loading some of his assets, presumably for Capital gains and/or Inheritance Tax purposes.

The total value of the holding in my possession was below the savings total allowed by those in receipt of Social Security benefits, so to date there had been no problem. They were not saleable on the open market anyway. However, they had a value. With the Inland Revenue's reassessment, the value would be placed well above the allowable limit for savings for those in receipt of Benefits. If my Benefits were withdrawn, and I was unable to sell the shares within the Company, I would have little or no income as my business was not yet profitable enough to support us. My only source of income, therefore, would be to sell these shares, if I could, and live off the proceeds. My Father would not be pleased. To have to live off the proceeds would have been anathema to him – a total waste of money in his eyes. The situation caused me a deal of worry.

The Company was a private limited one so selling the shares would have to be to other shareholders (assuming anyone wanted them), namely members of the family; my sibings, my Father's brothers or their families, or even to relatives further along the branches of the family tree. Selling them would defeat the reason my Father had given us the shares in the first place. Also, they had come to be shared among me and my siblings with a proviso – we were not, on any account, to sell any of the shares. There was obviously a certain amount of fraternal rivalry regarding control within the Company and my Father was determined to safeguard his family's interest in this humble empire.

The Conservatory

From where does my inspiration come? After a few restless nights, I had the most amazing 'Eureka' moment. As a business, we were operating in cramped, and far from ideal conditions. It was not ideal from the point of view of family life either. Divine inspiration seemed to be, as ever, with me. Whether my Father would be amenable to the same Divine input I was far from sure. My Father would not want the shares back as that would negate the reason for passing them on in the first place. So why not sell the shares to one (or more) of my siblings and invest the money in an extension to my property for use as an office? There was space at the rear of the bungalow and a conservatory would be an enhancement.

Somewhat gingerly, I put the proposal to my parents. My father was very much a 'concrete assets' man and not speculative by nature. He was third generation in this family business and had acquired his position as Director in the company as a filial privilege. The idea I put before him was that I had no option but to sell a portion of my shares in order not to lose my State Benefits. The next step would be to invest the money into bricks, mortar and, in this case, glass also. That way, I had the advantage of being able to expand my business sensibly, as well as enhance the value of my property – and not lose my current income. A win-win situation.

I hoped Dad would accept this logic as I would be preserving my meagre capital (albeit in bricks and mortar) which he had no wish to see diminished. Nor would he wish to fund me as an alternative means of income because there were five younger siblings whom he would wish to treat equally in the distribution of any advance inheritance.

My Father was, as anticipated, not very pleased. He had never approved of me setting up in business in the first place. I expect he thought that this was just one of the types of problems he had envisioned might be encountered in my attempt at earning my own income. To compound matters, none of my siblings was in a position to purchase the shares.

Financial Planning

Eventually my Father came back with a proposal. Mother would buy the shares from me. I believe it may have rather scuppered some of his financial planning, but as I was already up and running with my ambition to earn my own living, he could see the difficulty I was in and the logic of what I was proposing to get myself out of the muddle. If he did believe his earlier scepticism about me running a business, this time he made no negative comments.

Plans were drawn up for the conservatory and, not long after, we had a smart office at the back of the property with a doorway leading from my bedroom. We did consider turning my bedroom into the living room but a bedroom at the front, and lounge at the back of the bungalow did not seem to work because of the design of the property.

When the Social Security re-assessed me (as they did annually) I could honestly report that my savings were below the level above which I would have lost my benefits. The property one lived in, or any part of it, was not considered when assessing one's means.

A Dedicated Office

I now had a dedicated office that did not disrupt the children. The only exception was that staff had to pass by their bedrooms to get to it but, as they were generally at school during working hours, this did not represent much of a problem. The staff did have to pass through my bedroom which was at least encouragement for me to keep it tidy!

~

REFLECTION:

LATERAL THINKING

There is a saying: "There are no problems, only solutions."

When the paralyzed man was brought by his friends to Jesus for healing, they could get nowhere near Him for the throng of the crowds surrounding Him. But they didn't give up - they wanted to see their friend physically healed. So they clambered onto the roof of the place where Jesus was and dug a hole above Him, large enough for the paralytic, lying on his mat, to be lowered through (Mark 2:3-5). In Biblical times, of course, buildings would have been constructed of much simpler materials than they are nowadays. Imagine the trust the paralytic must have had in his friends in accepting their plan of action!

Would we undertake similar enterprises today? Why not, if it means achieving a goal that is vitally important to us? The paralytic's friends were duly rewarded for their perseverance and courage and their trust in the Lord's goodness. Not only was the paralysed man healed so that he was able to take up his mat and walk away, but first and foremost Jesus forgave him his sins. (Mark 2:11-12) His friends must have felt very jubilant at the outcome of the dual healing of their friend. Persistence achieves goals – and sometimes even additional rewards.

THOUGHTS FOR DISCUSSION

1. When a problem presents itself as insurmountable, do you: bury your head in the sand and do nothing because it seems impossible? Or;

2. Do you think outside the box to search for a solution – and have the persistence and courage to carry it through?

3. How important is trust in accepting help from others?

--ooOoo--

Chapter 6

BEHIND THE SCENES

A FATHER'S CONCERN

Interference

I was relieved that my Father had seen my business turn the corner and on the way to becoming successful before he died. He had not always been happy with my plans. Whilst I was still at College, I needed to replace the old Wolseley that had already lived way beyond its allotted lifespan. I found a second-hand Morris Marina that was to cost me the grand sum of £375, the best I could afford at the time. My Father got wind of what I was up to and was not happy.

Father was under the impression I did not need a car. Yet I had three children to run around to after-school activities, I was unable to carry much shopping because of my spinal problem, I was doing my evening class in Norwich (rural locations are not blessed with buses after 6pm) and I was planning to start a business. We also lived in a village, somewhat remote from many facilities, and seven miles distant from the centre of Norwich.

Dad particularly did not approve of me setting up in business. His Victorian idealism that had been fostered during his upbringing, and seemingly had never been updated, led him to believe that a woman's place was in the home, tending full-time to children and the housekeeping. He was totally out of touch with modern social mores.

I pointed out that in these modern times even single mothers were expected to contribute to the family's financial keep. The children were now all at senior school, therefore I agreed that it was time I earned my own living - even if my Father did not. I pointed out to him the many reasons why a car was necessary, including the fact I was planning to set up a business, but he insisted that "A mother should be at home looking after her children." He thought I was crazy to think of setting up in business – I presume he thought it would be another drain on my meagre resources and I would end up losing the roof over our heads.

The Row

I had just returned from my evening class at City College in Norwich which finished at 9.30pm, and was tired and hungry after the drive home. I had also to prepare for a trip, the following day, for a special surprise in London, arranged by my old school friend, Heather, as a belated 40th birthday celebration. I had assumed it would be a meal at some special venue as she had suggested I should dress smartly for the occasion.

My Father rang just after I arrived home. I ended up having quite an argument with him over the telephone, having to remind him that I was 40 years of age and quite capable of making my own decisions regarding purchasing a car, or undertaking anything else for that matter. I have never liked conflict but, to my surprise, I remained very confident of my plans. Eventually I managed to calm him down and a fragile truce ensued. We had been on the phone for over 90 minutes – his bill, thankfully. My nerves were pretty shot afterwards as I hate disagreements. I hastily had something to eat, prepared for my trip to London, and got to bed hoping to be up and ready for an early start in the morning.

The Birthday Treat

I was to meet my friend, Heather, at 11.30am under the clock at Victoria Station. After seeing the children off to school, I hurried to the station to catch my train. Somehow, in my befuddled state after the row, I arrived in London just after 11am thinking I had at least an hour to spare, so I wandered off around John Lewis to kill time. I presume my assumption it was to be a lunch date added to the confusion.

I arrived at Victoria Station an hour later, at 12.15, for once being quite proud I was 15 minutes early - time-keeping is not normally my strongest virtue. Within a few minutes my friend came running over in a frenzied state; "Where have you been?!" she exclaimed, "The train has gone!" She had only booked us a trip on the Orient Express for this belated 40th birthday treat! We were to have experienced a fabulous lunch served on board as we travelled through the Kent countryside – and I had blown it.

I didn't know where to put myself or how to apologise sufficiently. I offered to pay but secretly wondered whether I would be able to afford to as this sort of occasion was way out of my normal league. We wandered around London barely knowing how to talk to each other until the time for our return trains home.

If it had not been for the phone call from my Father the previous evening I would have had time to properly check my times and it was tempting to blame my Dad. I thought I had ruined my friendship with Heather for good as I did not hear from her again until the Christmas following. And when I did, I was overjoyed that our friendship was preserved. Not only had she managed to get a good portion of her money back (except the cost of the meal itself) - she had also rebooked the trip for the following year!! A true, forgiving, friend indeed!

A Father's Blessing

There was a blessed finale to that memorable phone call with my Father. Some months after that episode, and shortly after I had got my business up and running, I received another phone call from him. He was changing his car, and his ten-year-old Opel Berlina, a two-litre automatic, was not going to fetch much money – would I like it? This was a complete 'volte face' to his earlier thinking, and a double endorsement – he had finally given his blessing to my chosen way forward despite his earlier Victorian misgivings, and he had finally acknowledged my need for a car! I was delighted to finally have his approval.

The Limo

The car proved invaluable in more ways than one. It had an automatic gear box, it had a lovely smooth suspension and comfortable leather seats. Whether caused by the Marina or otherwise, I had found that driving was becoming more and more difficult and uncomfortable. It aggravated my spinal problem which seemed to be getting worse and creeping upwards. I had even begun to consider the possibility I might have to give up driving altogether. With the Opel, not having to change gears and operate a clutch was a big relief as were, of course, the comfortable seats and the smooth ride the car afforded. It felt as though I was driving a smart limousine despite its age. And despite its age too, it was in excellent condition and created a good image for the business.

FORAYS INTO TRAVEL ABROAD

Profit

By 1991, my accounts were starting to show a profit. Life was beginning to take on a new light. I had always had a great yen for travelling to foreign parts and I was beginning to earn the money to enable me to do so. I went on holiday abroad, not just once, but twice that year – the first being for an unexpected long weekend. The first should have been a family holiday to Malta scheduled for mid-July once the schools broke up. My children had never been abroad and I wanted to treat them before they all started leaving home. We found a reasonably priced holiday that left from Norwich Airport. However, the unscheduled intervening trip rather messed this up.

Majorca

A few weeks before our date of departure, my father, who adored his holidays, had travelled to Majorca with my Mother, accompanied by my youngest brother and his family. They were staying at their usual holiday venue, a flat in Paguera on the south-west coast of the island.

On the Monday of the second week of their holiday, my Father came out of the sea after his daily swim and complained of stomach pains. Only because he had a medical history, which included an operation for bladder cancer some 18 months earlier, did they take him to hospital. He had been given a clean bill of health at the beginning of the year by his Oncologist, and we had celebrated his 70th birthday in the February – ten months late.

My father lived for his holidays, and I don't believe he ever realised how much he regularly triggered my feelings of envy by raving on about the good times he and Mum had on their various holidays whenever I saw him. I had had years of going no further than the Norfolk coast, if we were lucky, when friends would offer us a tent, or a few days in their caravan. Like him, travel is in my blood, and I have a great desire to see the world.

Now that I was beginning to make some money, I was looking forward to some opportunities to indulge in this passion. As children, we were regularly taken across the Channel to visit our Belgian grandparents, including my Mother's large family of brothers, sisters, nephews and nieces - our aunts, uncles and cousins. The family name, Jongen, was Flemish, and I often wonder whether we had Dutch seafaring blood coursing through our veins as we were all very partial to coastal waters and sea travel.

My Father was kept in hospital for tests. On the Wednesday evening I received a phone call from my brother. Dad was having a life-or-death operation. Despite his Consultant's prognosis earlier in the year, the cancer had spread. He made it through the operation but he was not in a good state. My sister and I decided we should go and visit him with immediate effect. Her husband was organising our travel arrangements for the Friday and advised me to be prepared with bag packed and await instructions. He would ring and tell me whether I was to meet my sister in Nottingham where they lived, or at one of the airports.

Travel Traumas

On the Friday morning, I waited around as instructed for the phone call from my brother-in-law. By midday, I had heard nothing, so prepared a bowl of soup. The train times in all directions were safely in my jacket pocket. At ten minutes past twelve, just as I was spooning soup from bowl to mouth, the phone rang. Could I be at Gatwick for a flight that was due to leave at 5.30pm? This was cutting it fine, but I knew there was a train into Norwich at 12.35pm in time to catch the London train leaving at 13.05, so I hastened down to Brundall Station, soup unfinished.

As I stood on the platform, the train I was due to catch duly came through the station but did not stop. I was panic-stricken. I went to the Station Master and explained my predicament. He told me not to worry; he would arrange for the next train, which was scheduled to stop at the Brundall Gardens Halt further down the line, to make an unscheduled stop at Brundall first. This was not due at Brundall until 12.50 and it was a nine-minute run into Norwich – if all proceeded as normal. I would, if lucky, have barely six minutes to cross from the arrival platform to the London-bound departure one at the opposite end of the station.

With much relief, I made it on to the London train with a minute to spare. As I relaxed in my seat I began to think of the journey ahead. Two hours to London, then across on the underground to catch the train to Gatwick. Nobody seemed able to tell me how long this final leg of the train journey would take. Assuming it to be around 30 minutes, with luck on my side I should arrive at Gatwick around 4pm. These thoughts were mulling through my mind when I suddenly became aware the train had not moved. It was 13.15.

By 13.25 I was in panic mode once again. I found the Guard at the end of the train and, almost in tears, I asked what the problem was and told him my sorry tale. The building of the Norwich A47 Southern By-Pass was under way and a girder had been accidentally dropped on the line. It was due to be cleared in approximately ten minutes, so he told me.

At this point my thoughts were, is it worth continuing the journey? I might miss the flight. For all I knew, my Father might have already died. Money was still fairly tight – if I missed the 'plane could I spare any more money to re-book an air ticket – especially as I had just booked a family holiday? What about my sister who would be expecting to meet me? Would she carry on regardless if I didn't show up? The Guard was very sympathetic when he heard my tale. "I can ring your brother-in-law for you. He might be able to get a message to your sister." I was surprised to learn that train travel had advanced to the point where they had phones in the Guard's vans - this was before mobile phones had become the norm.

The train finally departed shortly after 13.40 – over thirty-five minutes late. The Guard came up to me and told me they would arrange a taxi to get me across London for my Gatwick train. As we approached London, however, he came up to me again and said that, as we were now almost into rush hour, he had reconsidered my options. As the roads would be too congested for a timely taxi ride, he thought the faster option would be for me to move to the front of the train in order to be able to get off quickly and make for the underground. Even he did not know the duration of the Gatwick leg of the journey.

Heart in mouth, I finally boarded the Gatwick train with still no idea of the duration of the journey. We were twenty minutes into the ride when, out in the open, the train came to a halt in what appeared to be some sort of marshalling yard. A further ten minutes later, we were told to disembark because the train had broken down! If someone had told me such a tale of so many negative incidents in one journey, I might have remained sceptical. The fact that it was such a vital journey made it seem even more amazingly beyond belief.

Having boarded a replacement train, we finally arrived at Gatwick at 4.20pm, much to my relief. Ten minutes to find my sister, and an hour to spare before the flight. I felt safe and much gratified. My sister, when I found her, however, was in a state of absolute panic. "Where have you been? – where have you been!!?" she exclaimed. "What's the problem?" I replied. "You are supposed to book in two hours before the flight!" I hadn't flown since I went to Jersey with my family as a teenager many years before, and was unaware of airport etiquette, especially as I had not done the booking, and had not even seen the tickets.

Despite my sister's agitation, there was no problem checking in, regardless of my late arrival. As we waited around for the flight, I related to her the sorry tale of my eventful journey – only to hear the announcement that the flight was also delayed by half an hour.

Meeting with Mum

On arrival in Palma we went straight to the Hospital. It was a private hospital up on the hill overlooking the Bay, as we were to discover the following day when we sat in the gardens between visiting times. Mum had been by herself all day as my brother and his family had been obliged to return home that morning because their holiday had come to an end. Mum had been sleeping on a couch in the waiting area since Monday, but that day she had been offered the use of a single room that had become available in the Hospital. My sister and I had no hotel booked, so my Mother suggested we attempt to procure a couple of pillows from the staff and we slept on the floor in her room with our raincoats as mattresses.

Mother was so hyped up that she talked non-stop. As we were settling for the night she continued talking incessantly, and then, without a moment's hesitation between, her snoring filled the room. What with worry about Dad, the snoring, and more particularly the hard floor and my fragile spine, I, for one, did not sleep much that night.

My sister and I wandered into town the following morning and, rather than book some accommodation, we decided to buy camping mats for the second, and final night of our stay. These created a marginal improvement on the previous night's sleep.

Father's Day

It was mid-June and beautifully warm. It was also Father's Day. Dad had briefly regained consciousness around Friday lunchtime before we arrived, but did not to do so again. We were advised, however, that it was possible he could hear us if we talked to him, which we did during the brief visiting periods. The remainder of the time we spent in the rather lovely hospital grounds, up on a hill above Palma, overlooking the fantastic views of the city, the Basilica, and the ships in the Bay. For me, who was so in need of a rest after two-and-a-half years of struggling to get my business off the ground, it would have been the perfect weekend break - but for the circumstances.

On Sunday, the three of us attended Mass in the Hospital Chapel. It was a very emotional time and I wasn't quite sure what I was praying for, or what I thought. We had another visit to see Dad, and a little more time in the Hospital garden where I found lying on the grass more comfortable than sitting on the benches because of my painful back. It was not long before my sister and I had to depart for our flight back to the UK late on the Sunday afternoon. The oldest of our three brothers was due to arrive that evening to be with Mum.

Back to Reality

On the Monday and Tuesday, I had to focus on my business as the end of the previous week had been rather disrupted. Wednesday was my birthday, but I was hardly in a mood to celebrate.

Before the day was over, I received the inevitable phone call that my Father had died. In a strange way, I felt rather privileged that my birthday was the date of his departure from this world, though my Mother found it hard to remember my birthday with any enthusiasm for years to come. The positive, if there is ever a positive when one loses someone close, is that he died doing what he enjoyed most. He was on holiday in his favourite resort, with the wife he adored, and his youngest son and family of whom he was particularly fond. Had he survived, he would have been an invalid for the remainder of his life, the prognosis for which was expected to be around six months. Both these facts would not have sat well with him at all. As a family, we are not able to cope well with illness or disability, as I was eventually to discover.

Malta

There was a problem I had to deal with now that my Father had died, and that was the long-awaited holiday with my children. It was due to commence within a few weeks and there was the funeral to consider. Fortunately, the holiday insurance covered a change of date because of the circumstances, and the holiday was rearranged for the last week in August. My parents, too, were well covered by their holiday insurance and my Father's body was flown back to the UK. As the oldest of the siblings, I had to prepare a eulogy for the funeral which I also translated and read in French for the members of my Mother's family who arrived from Belgium for the occasion.

The holiday in Malta was now two months after my Father's demise. The weather had been quite comfortable up on the hill in Palma in mid-June. When we arrived at Valetta I remember walking out from the air-conditioned Airport and behind a waiting bus, and thought I had met with its steamingly hot exhaust. I had never experienced Mediterranean holidays before, or indeed anything further south in the world than Jersey, so it was quite a surprise to find this excessive heat was not from the coach's exhaust at all, but it was the heat we were to experience for the remainder of the holiday. My son found it so intolerable, particularly at night, that he spent the whole week sleeping out on the balcony of our family room.

The children did, however, enjoy the cool of the waters whilst snorkelling and swimming and I had the difficulty of negotiating with them some interspersed days of cultural sight-seeing. The firework displays for the Feast of St Julian were an experience never to be forgotten. Stupendously beautiful fireworks were going off non-stop, in every direction - even on ships out at sea. The displays went on continuously from 6pm until about three or four in the morning. Millions of Maltese pounds must have gone up in smoke that night, as I believe it still does each year when this celebration takes place.

102

Israel

Why had I tried to find a career which would enable me to operate from home? Was I being unduly pessimistic about the future condition of my spine? After all, the symptoms, up to this point, were diagnosed as being a slipped disc and, more latterly, a sacro-ileac joint problem – approximately 50% of the population suffer such problems and most managed their lives relatively well regardless.

It seems that my negative thoughts on this subject were not totally unfounded. The following year, in October 1992, I decided to go on a parish pilgrimage to Israel. My spine failed me on the first day and I was in great discomfort, probably because I had attempted to mow the lawn prior to leaving.

It was on this trip that I learnt a lesson in accepting help. We were sitting on a wall outside the Dome of the Rock in Jerusalem, taking off our shoes before entering. Some kind fellow pilgrim offered to assist me with the removal of my sandals. I replied: "Thank you, but I can manage" which, evidently, I could, but not without an obvious struggle because of the painful state of my spine. I was told, very kindly but in no uncertain terms that, by refusing help, I was depriving the offeror the opportunity of enacting a kindness. By refusing offers of assistance, I had always assumed I was preventing people from being inconvenienced. I had not considered I was causing them a deprivation. Nowadays, with this lesson indelibly etched on my mind, I still must remind myself to say "Yes, thank you" when such offers come my way.

The pilgrimage visited many of the places that Jesus had frequented during His brief ministry on earth, included walking the Way of the Cross – a very moving experience. What amazed me also, was the distances Jesus and His disciples must have walked (which we thankfully travelled by air-conditioned coach), and the immense variations in the geography of the terrain – desert on one side of Jerusalem and resplendent verdure on the other - and the amazing Dead Sea, laden with salt, where you could float on the water reading a book, so long as you remembered not to rub your eyes. Historically, it was fascinating and quite something to see the places mentioned in the Bible in their reality. Even more amazing for me, was the fanciful idea that we were breathing the air Jesus would have breathed, though it had, of course, undergone nigh on two thousand years of recycling by the time it entered our lungs.

Abandoned

Among the many beautiful and poignant places we visited on this pilgrimage was a visit to Tabgha, a fairly isolated place on the edge of the Sea of Galilee where the feeding of the five thousand was purported to have taken place. On re-boarding the coach for our return to the hotel for lunch, our Leader did his usual head count by asking each of us to make sure we had our travelling companion in the seat beside us.

One elderly lady was holidaying with her sister and, having been a widow for many years, she had obviously travelled a lot on her own. We were twenty minutes on the drive back to the hotel when this dear lady realised her sister was not on board. The coach turned around to find her. Another twenty minutes further on, this poor lady was discovered wandering down the road in the midday heat which, even in October, could reach up to 30C. She was rather anxious and somewhat fazed, but apparently reasonably confident she would not be entirely forgotten. By the very essence of the pilgrimage, I feel sure it would not have been too long before the frosty reuniting of the abandoned lady with her sister would soon have melted as she forgave her for 'forgetting' her in the boiling heat of the day.

We also visited the Pool at Bethesda where, in biblical times, many were purported to be healed by being the first to enter the waters when they became 'troubled'. It was here that Jesus healed the cripple who was never able to reach the water in time to be first in. I had a vague optimism that I, too, might be rid of my spinal problem if I could get near the water. I was most put out when our leader considered I should wait at the top because of the unevenness of the terrain, and I watched ruefully as the rest of the party disappeared down the rocky path to visit the well. If anyone in the party needed a chance to be healed by the waters, it was me!

~

REFLECTION:

THE FATHER'S LOVE

Sometimes earthly fathers can be over-protective and do not know when or how to 'let go'. They find it hard to give up their active parenting role despite years of coaching us to develop into the sensible independent adults that hopefully we have become. This inability to reduce their responsibilities despite our adulthood may be through force of habit, maybe through fear of feeling redundant as a parent, or maybe simply because of the intense love they have for us and wanting to keep us close. Earthly fathers can be fallible and only discernment can guide us whether to follow their advice or not – the discernment that comes via the Holy Spirit.

Our Heavenly Father operates differently. In His perfect wisdom, He gave us, via Moses, a simple, but all-encompassing set of rules (the Ten Commandments) - and the complete freedom to follow them or not as we choose. He gave us free will - He knows how to 'let go'.

When the humanity He created seemed not to be making a good fist of things, He even sent His Beloved Son to tease out further for us, by word and witness, how we should better interpret these rules. He desperately wants us to love Him as He loves us, but by reciprocity, not coercion.

Regardless of how we act upon the freedom He has given us, He never lets go of His love for us - it is there waiting in the background for us to discover its full depth and intensity. He knows us through and through, even to every hair on our heads (Luke 12:6-7) and is ready to welcome us whatever our sinful status. In the parable of the prodigal son, Jesus gave an example of the joy the Father feels when an errant son returns after a length of time spent wasting his inheritance through a life of debauchery. The prodigal returns to his father in humility and is welcomed with open arms and celebration. This is as our Heavenly Father does when we transgress and turn back to Him (Luke 15:11-24).

Before He left this earth, Jesus promised He would send His Holy Spirit for continued guidance (John 14:26). We are free to call on Him. And it is through His Holy Spirit that we learn discernment.

THOUGHTS FOR DISCUSSION

1. Many have behaved in a similar manner to the prodigal son but do not believe that God, their Heavenly Father, would ever forgive them. Could you persuade them otherwise?

2. God's Holy Spirit is a source of empowerment frequently overlooked in people's lives. He offers us guidance through the teachings of Jesus and His Father, and far more besides. How often do you feel His influence in your life?

3. How easy is it to call on the Holy Spirit for guidance?

--ooOoo--

Chapter 7

RUNNING HERON

INVENTORY INCIDENTS

Our Inventories

Unlike many agencies, I always encouraged a very detailed inventory which we carried out for the landlord as part of the administration fee. We charged a slightly higher monthly management fee than most agencies but it was all inclusive, and there was no initial up-front fee. It had the benefit of simplifying the accounting. However, the landlords were committed to a minimum twelve months of our management service or they forfeited the balance of the first year's fees.

Besides being very detailed, the inventories included any noticeable marks on walls or furniture, etc. We did exclude loft contents partly because I had no head for heights and I was usually the one who compiled the inventories! If a landlord left anything in his/her loft, then it was their liability if anything went missing. Initially we included garage contents and garden items but eventually these were charged as an extra if the landlord wished for these to be included.

Pet Possessions

However detailed the inventory, you could guarantee there would be some issue of grievance. Having meticulously compiled such an inventory for a landlord who was going abroad (which included the very precious pet cat that was to be left behind!), I omitted to include a very rusty old cartwheel that was propped up against the shed at the bottom of the rather rambling garden that backed onto a field, beyond which was the Norwich to Great Yarmouth/Lowestoft railway line. On his return, some three years later, the landlord was most upset to find this battered and time-worn cartwheel had disappeared.

I was more concerned about taking on the responsibility of their valuable, over-indulged cat. This was quite an undertaking on our part because if the property remained empty between tenancies, the cat, Mercedes - a six-year-old Persian, had to be taken by us to her regular cattery. I hadn't considered this unique request to be part of our specialist service, but what, otherwise, would become of her? Mercedes's owners were a childless couple and she was their prized possession, and treated royally as their substitute offspring.

Mercedes

It was quite an honour to think that we were to be entrusted with this treasured cat's care, but it would not be easy, firstly to find cat-loving tenants, and, moreover, tenants who would be prepared to care for her as part of their tenancy conditions. But was I not offering a specialist homecare service?

The family who applied for the first tenancy were, thankfully, approved by the landlords before they left for Russia. The prospective tenants had a couple of cats of their own and, having met Mercedes, were happy to take her on. Three days after they moved in I received a phone call from the tenants. Mercedes's body had been found by the railway line. She had disappeared the day after they moved in.

I wrote to the landlords in trepidation to explain what had happened. I received no reply. In the office, we decided that Mercedes had either taken a dislike to the pair of feline intruders who had invaded her personal territory or, possibly, she missed her owner/parents and

108

committed suicide out of despair at their abandonment of her. When the landlords returned some three years later, as I said, they were more concerned about the missing, rusted cartwheel and nothing was said about the deceased Mercedes.

The White Glove Test

It was not too many months after I started the business that I found I needed assistance. My first assistant was an ex-RAF friend-of-a-friend who had been 'early-retired' from Norwich's famous engineering firm, Lawrence-Scott Electromotors. He lived locally and was prepared to work on an 'as-needed' basis so I could call on him whenever I had a viewing or inspection to be carried out. This was very handy as it saved paying a set wage while times were still tough trying to earn a living income for my own family needs.

John displayed his RAF training in many ways. He was the perfect gentleman, and ideal for doing property inspections using the renowned RAF 'white-glove' test for checking that a property was in a fit state for hand-back after a tenancy. The 'white glove' test involves inspecting that no dust is left, even in the more obscure places such as above door lintels or in corners of floors, etc., the white glove giving evidence if such remained. If so, tenants would be obliged to do a re-clean.

At these check-out inspections, at which a member of staff always attended, the detailed inventory was checked to ensure everything was present in the way it had been signed for by the tenant at check-in. Ovens, grills, toilets and cupboards were thoroughly inspected, as were the furniture and mattresses. Carpets had to be cleaned, and if the landlord had agreed to pets (for which an additional deposit was required), then an anti-flea solution had to be added to the carpet cleaning fluid. The 'white glove' inspection followed. Successfully concluded, and with the landlord's approval – preferably after a personal inspection by him or herself – then, and only then, was the deposit returned to the tenant.

Beasts That Bite

On one occasion, one of my later colleagues who had been carrying out a check-out inspection, arrived back at the office in a state. Her legs, in particular, and other parts of her body, were almost completely covered in small angry-looking lumps. I sent her home for a bath and fresh clothing and told her to take the rest of the day off. The out-going tenant, with his dog, had left the premises prior to the inspection without cleaning the carpets, therefore no flea deterrent had been used either.

Fleas live off a host, quite often on a domestic pet, probably picked up when out for walks in the wild, and they lay their eggs in the carpets. Once hatched, the new-born fleas search for a host – usually the household pet cat or dog. When a pet leaves a property, the hatching fleas are left with no animal to feed off. The fleas turn to the first living creature that enters the property, human or otherwise, and a banquet ensues by the near-starved fleas. In this case, my colleague had unwittingly provided the feast.

Many of our tenant pet owners seemed totally unaware of the habits of the leeching creatures that nestled in their pets' fur coating and often railed at the fact they had to add a flea deterrent, and even at being obliged to clean the carpets at all. My poor colleague had become one of their victims.

EQUIPMENT

Landline

Among the handful of my first landlords, three of them resided abroad; in Canada, Russia, and Hong Kong. I had to accept the fact that there were going to be expensive phone calls to be made as the early 'nineties were still in the pre mobile phone, texting and emailing era. The Telex had given way to fax machines of which I was soon to make an investment, and this helped for non-urgent messaging. We added an additional 2% to the monthly management charge for landlords living overseas to cover the additional costs of communicating; postage for documents requiring signature, phone calls, etc.

If there were urgent decisions to be made re maintenance issues and the like, the phone was often the essential tool. It was quite frustrating at times: my very first landlord, the Cathay-Pacific airline pilot living in Hong Kong, was one of the most difficult to get hold of. I would have to wait up until 1am to catch either him or his wife at 9am Hong Kong time. Inevitably, their maid would answer the phone with the consequent "I'll just get Mr S….. for you".

After some delay, the said landlord, assuming he was not piloting a Boeing 747, would arrive on the phone and there would be the usual niceties of discussing the weather - regardless of the oceans and landmasses that divided us. Finally, we would get down to the business of the day (in my case the night!) and "I'll just have a chat with the wife to see what she thinks". Some moments further on, and an even more expensive phone bill later, a decision would finally reach my ears.

I often wondered how other letting agencies, assuming they had any overseas landlords, managed urgent matters affecting them. Maybe they had an open mandate for simply getting on with essential repairs and maintenance, regardless of cause. I felt this could be open to abuse and much preferred my landlords' consent before spending their money, rather than doing so without their knowledge.

First investments

My first investment was, of course, a computer as I could not continue using my neighbour's indefinitely, especially as it was becoming used for most of the day, every day. Without a computer, I was hand-typing tenancy agreements.

A second-hand Delta Gold was the first computer I bought for the princely sum of £2,400 – this was the beginning of the 1990s! The tenancy agreements that previously I had been hand-typing – each one seven pages - could now be saved. All that needed to be altered on the computer for each new tenancy were just a few words, such as date, owner's and tenant's names, the property to be let and the landlord's address, and maybe the odd change of clause.

The fax machine, bought a couple of years later, was a mere £240 in comparison. This enabled us to fax agreements abroad and to received them faxed back duly signed.

Mobile Phone

Mobile phones in the form of car phones were the next innovation to come onto the market but they were incredibly heavy, the weight of bricks, and mostly used by sales people on the move.

I finally invested in a mobile phone after a horrendous journey to York to visit my son who had just begun to study for his PhD at the University where he had done his MSc during the previous four years. He had recently married at the tender age of twenty-one, and a great benefit to me was that he was to be supported in part by BT for

112

his PhD (they had sponsored the whole of his four-year MSc course), and partly also by his new wife who had found herself a teaching post in the area.

My journey was scheduled for a Friday afternoon. The previous day Leeds had been cut off by snow and I rang my son to discuss the wisdom of travelling in view of the weather conditions. "No worries, Mum, York is in a valley so we are fine". He was quite a weather expert having studied satellites, GPS, and other skyward interests as part of his degree. Being somewhat cautious, I set off in daylight, taking advantage of my freedom to manage my own time. I had advised my daughter-in-law, who arrived home from school around 4.30pm, that she could expect me to arrive soon after.

Snow was beginning to fall lightly as I left and I carried a mental image of where the hotels and stop-overs might be along the way in case of difficulty. I had planned to go via the Humber Bridge for a change, instead of up the A1, and this took me via Lincoln. The snow had become somewhat heavier the further along the route I progressed. When I got to this fine city, built on a hill and topped by a magnificent cathedral, cars were sliding all over the roads and beginning to clog up the city. I decided on a change of course and turned back towards the A1, the route I was familiar with.

The snow was now quite deep and progress was slow as vehicles followed each other in the ruts created by the ones in front. Eventually I reached the A1. It was 4pm – too early to stop and call my daughter-in-law to tell her of the delay as I was still nearly two hours away. Instead, I would continue on my way and stop to phone her at one of the roadside services.

Not a very few miles along the A1, a strange event occurred. It had begun to rain by this time, and darkness was descending. To begin with, we travelled very slowly because of the slush conditions. The

113

snow had almost completely disappeared as the rain grew heavier and heavier, when unexpectedly all the traffic came to a complete halt.

Nothing moved, and it was difficult to understand what was causing the hold-up. We were near a slip road and rush-hour traffic attempting to join the A1 was also at a standstill. Everything appeared to be in complete chaos with nothing moving except the pouring rain. I turned on the radio but there was no news of what was going on.

Despite being wedged between vehicles full of humanity, not merely behind and in front, but beside also, it was quite a scary experience. I felt trapped. I turned the radio up louder for company but it didn't help. There was total darkness except for headlights, and stationery vehicles everywhere. I thought my family would be very worried by now as the snow had all disappeared and heavy rain had taken its place.

Nearly an hour and three quarters later we finally started to move and I pulled into the nearest service station – along with a myriad other north-bound travellers. The queue for the one and only public phone was approximately 40 persons deep and people with journeys disrupted by the day's weather conditions were calling out for lifts to various parts of the country. The southern part of Britain had been the worse to experience the blizzard conditions.

Among the many voices babbling away about their experiences and worries about their continued travel, I heard someone call "Is anyone going to York?" Without thinking I responded positively. It was a young soldier. My thoughts were "What have I done?!" I, a woman on her own, had offered to be accompanied on my further travel by a complete stranger, and a male at that!

We had a coffee together and I learnt he had been travelling all day from Dover on cadged lifts because of cancelled or disrupted trains due to the snow. He seemed a nice enough guy and anyway, in the circumstances, I did not feel I could back out of my offer. Eventually I was able to make my phone call to reassure the family and we finally set off on our way to complete the rest of our journey trouble-free. The chaos was apparently caused by a lorry that had jack-knifed earlier in the day in the snow on a hill a long way up the A1 causing the massive tail-back.

To be honest, it was a great relief to have a travelling companion. Even more so, as he knew exactly where to find my son's new address, so he guided me through the streets of York safely to my destination. It was not long after that I became the proud owner of a Nokia mobile. By 1995, mobile phones had, thankfully, greatly reduced in size from the bulky car phones of earlier years.

A mobile made such a difference to being out on the road during the course of work. If one of my clients rang the office to inform us they were delayed after I had already left to attend the appointment, or they needed to cancel an appointment, I could receive forwarded messages to my mobile so that unnecessary time wastage on abortive visits was minimised.

Key Safe

We developed a key system whereby the property number and first two letters of its road name was put on the back of each label for our identification. In many cases the properties had house names instead of numbers. The same rule applied; the first two letters of the house name (excluding any reference to 'The' ...) was again followed by the first two letters of the road name. The reverse of the label bore our address and phone number.

Two sets of keys were requested from each landlord. One, the full set, was for handing to an incoming tenant; the second set was used by us for access. This was kept in our key safe for emergencies, or for when a tenant had given permission for us to enter the property in their absence for an inspection or maintenance purposes. The tenants' sets bore dark green tags, the office sets had light green ones - green being our corporate colour.

This system proved invaluable on an occasion when I had my briefcase stolen. The case, minus contents, was found in a waste bin near the Norfolk and Norwich hospital in Norwich, about a mile from the scene of the theft. Many months later I received a phone call from a man who announced that he had found a set of keys with our address whilst trimming his hedge at his home not far from the railway station. This was two miles in a completely different direction from where the briefcase had been found. The keys could not be identified against any property and they had been ditched by the thief in disgust. We got the keys back, thanks to our labelling system.

Faith and Trust

I discovered that something more valuable than material equipment had been an essential tool for the foundation and on-going energy of my business - something I could not touch, hold, feel or see – other than with an inner eye. Faith. What was it that gave me that new-found inner strength and confidence to set up this business and keep it going? What spurred me on to take the risks I did? What spurred me to carry on, even when my disability worsened to the point when truly I should not have continued managing so many properties that, in most cases, were my landlords' most major investments? Who was it that sorted out the problems: the accidental double-bookings when either one of my valuable clients could have taken serious offence if we cancelled; or I (or my staff) had inadvertently breached some legality we were unaware of? Or the emergency at a property we were unsure how to handle? Nobody can say that any business runs smoothly all the time. Yet daily, solutions materialised to problems that it was difficult to envisage in advance how they might become resolved.

All these things occurred quite frequently. They got sorted with a regularity that very soon gave me the confidence not to worry when such crises reared their ugly heads. I would simply say "Lord, this is YOUR business that you have entrusted to me. I have had no proper training; I certainly could not have started it without Your help. I know there will come a time when I will have to give it up, but if it is Your will that I continue now, I hand over this problem for You to sort." And always, before the day was out, there would be a solution. I knew that some day I would receive a strong indicator that it was time to give up – I just hoped and prayed that it would not be because of an unsolvable crisis that caused me to fall flat on my face – and, despite my lack of proper training, I was even saved from that.

SAFETY

Staff and Trust

I had some quite valuable properties under my care and, importantly, many were the landlords' homes to which they wished to return at some later stage. Trust was, therefore, an important element in my business. It was vital that we chose sensible trustworthy clients to rent them.

It also required trustworthy staff on whom I could rely to ensure the properties were locked up properly after each visit, and that all was well, and nothing missed at an inspection such as leaks or essential maintenance. If a property was left empty in winter it was important that water and power were attended to according to landlord's instructions. Usually the utilities were turned off, unless the landlord was prepared to take over the cost of the heating for the duration the property remained empty.

Another important aspect in choosing staff was compatibility which, to me, was as important as their skills. They were, after all, working in my home. Even after we moved, not only were they using the office which had its own kitchen but they required access through the interconnecting door to my home for cloakroom facilities.

Feeling comfortable with my staff became more important as my disability increased, as occasionally I needed assistance in certain areas of daily living. Not least, also, was the fact that we shared the office space for 8.5 hours of the day and for 3 hours on Saturdays.

Despite retaining sole ownership of the business (except when Heron went 'limited' and my son became a 1% shareholder as a director), I frequently refer to events and decisions connected to the business as emanating from "we" instead of "I". Without the various loyal and trustworthy staff who remained in my employ over time, I could not have succeeded. Therefore, often, they were included in the decision-making.

Staff Safety – In the Office

Another aspect of safety was protection for the staff, particularly in case of unsavoury visitors. Because the 'office' was inside my home (and later attached to it when, as a garage, I gained special planning permission for its conversion), clients were not encouraged to visit. New landlords, and applicants wishing to rent, would be met at the property and all negotiations and paperwork would be mostly done on the spot.

Very occasionally, however, some would turn up at the office: an applicant who didn't have all the monies required at the viewing; or his/her partner was not able to be present with them at the viewing but they needed to sign documents; or a tenant wishing to pay their rent in cash – and who were we to turn money away! It was not possible to run a business such as this and for people not to know our address - it was a legal requirement.

Occasionally there were problems with those who did visit: an applicant whom the landlord had rejected in favour of someone more suitable; a tenant who was in dispute about deductions from a deposit; the possibility of a stranger up to some mischief?

I had a community alarm installed in the house, mainly for my personal use, but I informed the staff that if there was any sign of trouble they were to retreat out of the office into the hall, lock the intercommunicating door, and press the button for assistance. Fortunately, on the one and only occasion I recall a tenant using very threatening behaviour, I happened to be in the office. The whole family seemed to be present, of which three became quite menacing. We came very close to calling the police but we managed to persuade them to calm down, and eventually they left.

I even had one of the more chauvinistic landlords who became very aggressive towards me when I referred him to a clause in his landlord's agreement that he had signed that obliged him to pay some additional monies. He informed me that he had not taken the contract seriously and was not prepared to abide by the clause that was at the root of this disagreement. The implication was that I was running a 'Mickey Mouse' enterprise and was not to be taken seriously. Yet I am sure he expected his property to be properly looked after and, no doubt, he would have been equally aggressive had I not taken that responsibility with the full attention it deserved.

Safety – Away from the Office

There was also regard to the safety of staff when out and about – including myself. We were visiting properties, and meeting new landlords about whom we knew very little. We were also meeting, checking in, and inspecting properties inhabited by tenants. With the latter, we at least had some record of good character from the independent credit checks and references that were carried out.

Whether it was from a sixth sense or some form of intuition, I could summarise fairly accurately the type of person we were dealing with and whether they would be suitable for a particular landlord's property – even from a phone conversation. Members of staff were trained to ask all the pertinent questions over the phone and relay them to me before we decided whether to meet someone at a property. With a relaxed, friendly attitude it was quite easy to extract information from an applicant that helped identify the type of person we were likely to be meeting. Without fail, a name and telephone number of the person we would be meeting was to be recorded in the diary. Safety became better guaranteed, however, with the advent of the mobile phone.

Safety and Security - Properties

The high standard of the properties under Heron's care was one of the factors for which it became famous. This did not apply just to the state of cleanliness when the tenants left, but I was also very particular about how the landlords handed the properties over to me in the first place. There were quite a few I had to turn away, especially in the early days, either because they were too untidy, unclean, or even unsafe, and the landlords were not prepared to do anything to bring them up to a decent standard.

Historically, landlords had the upper hand. Before the 1988 Housing Act, supply did not meet demand, partly because owners of property had become nervous of renting out their investments because they could not be assured of regaining possession if tenants defaulted on their rent payments – in which case 'investment' property became something of a misnomer. Because of the shortage of property rentals, therefore, tenants were prepared to take whatever was available - regardless of condition - to ensure a roof over their heads. This attitude spilled over into the new era, post 1988, for a short while at least.

Safety Regulations

I came on the lettings scene with the attitude that tenants had as much right to have a decent standard of living as anyone else. As the years progressed, and letting became even more popular, legislation followed my standards. Safety regulations were introduced regarding fire and furnishings which came into effect in 1993, and for gas and electricity in 1994, to improve safety for tenants. I also encouraged smoke alarms to be installed in the properties for rent – these were only mandatory in houses of multiple occupancy during the time I was trading. It was not until October 2015 when a new Act was brought in making smoke detectors and monoxide detectors mandatory in every rented property.

HAZARDS

The Inexperienced Young

We had one case where a young man came home to the property he was renting from us after a night out of heavy drinking. He placed some bread under the grill to toast and threw himself onto his bed in a drunken haze. Fortunately, his neighbour got up in the night to use the bathroom, heard the smoke alarm and smelt the smoke transferring out from a window of the young man's flat and in through his open bathroom window. He thumped on the young man's door and eventually woke him, and he managed to escape. Thankfully he suffered little more than some smoke inhalation, and the anger of his Mother who had acted as his guarantor, and who had to cough up to make good the damage to the flat.

Quite frequently, tenants would remove the batteries from these alarms because they 'go off too often' – my children were equal culprits as they frequently set off the one outside my kitchen door. I reminded them that the minor noise inconvenience was nothing compared to the danger and trauma of having a house fire. There are ways and means of ensuring the alarm does not go off unnecessarily, such as shutting the kitchen door before opening a hot and dirty oven, not letting pans boil over, etc. Quite often the problem with younger people is their inexperience in these matters.

Some young tenants rang me one day to say their lights had gone out – was it a power cut? Not living in their area I could not say, but I took them through some suggestions as to how to find out. It turned out that other electrical equipment was functioning in the property so definitely not a power cut! Have you checked your fuse box? Despite its whereabouts being listed on their inventory, they had no clue as to where it was, or what it was, let alone how to fix the contents.

Money Meanness

One series of safety cases I recall involved the husband of someone I was well acquainted with who lived in the same village as I. He wanted me to manage a property of his near Norwich Airport. It attracted mainly KLM students who were training at the airport. Normally I did not take on student lettings as it was fraught with problems, but these were largely career students, past university age – and the landlord was the husband of someone I knew quite well.

On visiting the property, my first impression was this was a property I would normally turn away. It needed decorating, it needed curtains, it had a mis-match of furniture, it had a hatchway with sliding glass doors that had a missing protective plastic disc needed for opening and closing the hatch. Maybe, with a little persuasion, I could convince this landlord of the need to upgrade his property; after all he lived in a five-bedroomed property himself - with a swimming pool. He had no good reason not to improve his investment.

First there were the essentials. This was to be a furnished let yet he could not understand why the property needed curtains. Even for unfurnished lets, the minimum expectation would be for the property to have carpets or some form of floor covering, and curtains or blinds. The reason was all down to sizing. For people regularly on the move, as most renters are, it is quite unreasonable, even for those who can afford them, to expect tenants to provide their own curtains and carpets as these furnishings are unlikely to fit different houses or flats when they moved on.

This man was the archetypal, old-style landlord – his attitude was that as these tenants were only students (and mainly foreigners), they could manage without curtains. Then I broached the subject of the unsafe glass sliding doors of the hatchway with the missing plastic protector. He could not see the need for replacing this either. As I pointed out to him, if someone put their finger through the hole to pull the glass across, the two glass sliding doors would act like a guillotine and could chop off their finger.

Non-essential, but still quite necessary, was the state of the kitchen where fitted cupboards had been moved about and the consequent damaged walls had not been made good. There were leak stains and grease stains on what paintwork was visible, and the décor was therefore in great need of perking up. I offered to get a decorator to quote. No, no, he would redecorate it himself. The result was little better. He had evidently found half a dozen tins of left-over paint in his garage and used them up on the kitchen, resulting in the wall areas being covered in various colours. At least he had refreshed the paintwork as promised!

More seriously, some time later, I noticed three strip lights in the car port which, although working, were so badly rusted that they were in danger of falling, if not on someone's head, then on a tenant's car. I had to threaten him with refusing to manage the property further before he finally replaced the light fittings.

Management Manoeuvers

At a later stage, this same landlord took over the management of his own properties, presumably in the expectation it would halt any further nagging from me. He opted for our 'Setting-up Only' service whereby we advertised for tenants, carried out the credit checks, and arranged the tenancy agreements.

As already mentioned, the Law had, by this time, caught up with my ideals, and electrical, and gas safety checks had become mandatory. Even with the task of only setting up a tenancy for the landlord, the agent was responsible, in law, for making sure the property was safe, and had the prerequisite certificates, before allowing a tenant to take possession.

On this occasion, we found a pleasant young girl to take on this landlord's property located in Brundall - a 1960's one-bedroomed flat. We chased up the landlord for his gas certificate, and even offered to get the safety inspection done for him, but he insisted he wanted to arrange the inspection himself. Three times my colleague chased him up for the elusive certificate. On the fourth occasion, he told us he was leaving the certificate at the property for the incoming tenant. It was not part of our brief with the Set-up only (non-management) service for us to check the tenant into the property.

There comes a point where one should trust a person who is a well-known member of the local community, with executive employment in a large nationwide company. He was wealthy enough to own several rental properties beside his own sizeable home.

Six months from taking up the tenancy, this young girl telephoned the office. I told her we didn't manage the property and, if she had any issues, she needed to contact her landlord direct. She explained that she thought we ought to know that she had just returned from the doctors where she had been diagnosed with the beginnings of carbon monoxide poisoning. I referred her to her gas safety certificate and again reiterated that she needed to take up the matter urgently with her landlord. She explained she had never received a gas safety certificate. My heart lurched.

This landlord had lied to us and, not only had he risked a fine and/or imprisonment for himself, but he had also put my reputation on the line. More importantly he had endangered his tenant's life, all for the sake of the cost of some £70 for a gas safety inspection and certificate. I could have ended up, myself, with a £5,000 fine, and/or six months in jail, as agent for failing to ensure a valid certificate was in place before letting a property.

Needless to say, I had reached the end of my patience with this landlord and refused to accept any more business from him. The tenant, who was fortunately very forgiving, took the matter no further - and thankfully suffered no lasting health issues.

The Chiassy Case

During my business years, only once did my sixth sense fail me in my judgement of prospective tenants. We received a call one day from an Iranian academic doctor attached to Cambridge University who wished to rent a property in a quiet location in order to complete a thesis.

There were a couple of unusual circumstances about this applicant's request whereby, in normal circumstances, we would have rejected the applicant. He had come from Germany so we would be unable to check his references in the usual manner (the insurers were only able to validate a tenant with references generated from within the UK). Secondly, this prospective tenant wanted to rent for only a couple of months and our minimum term, to qualify under the contractual terms with our landlords, based on the 1988 Housing Act, was six months. However, we had recently taken on a property which seemed to be the most suitable for the Doctor's needs and it happened to be owned by a very amenable landlord.

I personally met Dr Chiassy at the property to show him around. He was very smartly dressed and a charming man. I put forward an account of my appraisal of him to the landlord in the best, unpersuasive manner I could muster. I was duty-bound to point out the possible negative outcomes of not having proper references, etc. but the landlord chose to take the risk, presumably because the Doctor's standing, and he agreed to allow him into his property.

As the Doctor intended to be at the property for only two months, he asked if the landlord would consider keeping the telephone account in his own name to save unnecessary complications - to which the landlord also agreed.

Bad Judgement

At this time, I had a male colleague who had designs on becoming a partner. It was he who did the check-in of our Iranian Doctor. One thing I always emphasised to my staff was that keys were never to be handed over to a tenant until the full sum of the first month's rent and the deposit had been received. My colleague arrived back from this check-in minus a third of the deposit. I was more annoyed that the rules had been disobeyed rather than any thoughts that the money would not shortly be made good by the tenant.

The following day the promise of the balance monies did not materialise. Instead, we received a phone call from the newly installed tenant, complaining about various things that he deemed

126

were not right at the property. It was evident these were trumped up excuses as the property belonged to a very caring and affable landlord, and, given our high standards, it was judged by us to be in very good order. The tenant duly paid some of the next month's rent and most of the following one, but he always remained partially in arrears and never made up the difference on his deposit.

Without permission, his agreed stay extended beyond the original two months and no further rent was received from him. The overdue monies mounted up as did our persistent chasing of it, but always there was an excuse. Finally, I decided to call at the property to confront the Doctor face-to-face. There was no trace of him – he had done a moonlight flit. When I got back to the office I phoned the University at Cambridge that he had provided as a contact – they had never heard of a Dr Chiassy. I traced the car registration number that was on his application form - it was a hired car. I phoned the hire company and they too had been left with an outstanding debt by our Doctor.

We had been scammed. I felt very badly that I had all but convinced the landlord he was a worthy candidate to take on, despite the unusual circumstances. The landlord, fortunately, was very understanding and sympathetic but I felt duty-bound to continue my pursuit of the man to make good the outstanding monies due to our landlord.

Nasty Surprises

Some three months later I was half-listening to the Ten O'clock News on ITV when I caught the name 'Chiassy' attached to an item regarding a parcel bomb that had been found at the TNT depot in Thetford. I immediately became more alert. This same person, an Iranian, had previously sent a letter bomb to a solicitor in Edinburgh who had sustained injuries to his hands, albeit fairly minor. The reason the bomb was sent? The solicitor had been pursuing this man named Chiassy for money. The news item closed with a request for any information regarding this person to be phoned through to the Police.

I immediately went into panic mode. There could not have been many persons in this country with such an unusual name as 'Chiassy', let alone one who was also Iranian. This was all too much of a coincidence. If it was the same person, I, too, was chasing him for money and a letter bomb could be winging its way to us also. The parcel intercepted at the TNT depot might, indeed, have been the very item intended to achieve the dastardly deed. I rang the Police.

The girl I spoke to was very sympathetic, and after a long period of listening as I related my experiences, she concluded with the comment that I had provided the most information so far. Could she send a couple of detectives around to take a statement?

Delighted Detectives

It was arranged that the detectives should come around the following Sunday afternoon and, after three hours, they finally concluded their questioning. They assumed Chiassy had fled the country on the day the parcel bomb at the TNT depot had been found. Just before leaving, the detectives asked me to let them know should I remember any further information, however seemingly trivial – names he may have mentioned, phone numbers, places or people he may have had contact with…. When they mentioned phone numbers I suddenly recalled we had the outstanding, itemised, phone bill. The detectives reacted like a pair of over-excited school boys!

As far as we were aware, the Police investigations came to nothing. The landlord was very laid back about the money he had lost. In fact, he seemed quite intrigued that his property had been the centre of so much attention. The staff at my office were less animated. Every time the postman arrived with the mail, they would tell him, if he had a parcel, he was to leave it no closer than the top of the drive. They were convinced our Iranian 'friend' was still capable of carrying out his evil deeds from across the water – or from wherever he might be lying low.

The local Press had picked up on the story – not from our point of view but from a Wroxham agent who had let a property to Chiassy the previous year. He had left this agency also in the lurch regarding outstanding payments. I was not keen to make any publicity from the event as I saw it rather as a failure of our normal high standards of thoroughly vetting our tenants - and of my judgement of character which had, for once, failed me.

The Guiding Guardian

Who ensured our safety in these situations? Who ensured my landlord in this, and the tenant in the previous case, would be so amenable and non-litigious, and that my reputation should remain undamaged? I had fortuitously avoided imprisonment and/or fine for issuing a tenancy agreement without a gas safety certificate, and, in the latter case, we were not harmed by a malicious letter or parcel bomb, or other damage from this sad foreigner.

STRANGE INHABITANTS

Reptilia

Some of our tenant applicants had bizarre requests when applying to rent properties. One, in particular, seemed obsessed about the heating in the bedrooms – what sort of temperature could be achieved? Could it be raised very high, around 28C? After much hedging, it transpired that he had a menagerie of some twenty-seven snakes that required high temperatures in order to survive. "They are all in glass tanks" says he. The landlord was not impressed, and we were rather relieved that he refused to accept this applicant with his slimy entourage.

Pythonidae

On another occasion, we had a very similar request; this time for one snake, a rather larger one – a pet python. As I was showing the applicant around this particular property, I thought he was joking when he announced that he had such a creature as a pet. He was desperate to find accommodation for himself and said python. He insisted that the python was harmless and begged me to ask the landlord if he would permit it in his property.

I spoke to the landlord who was a great procrastinator, always verbally weighing up the pros and cons, even of very minor situations, before arriving at a decision. "Well… I don't see why not. I've lived with the beasts when I was in Africa…" and he continued to ramble on about the domestic habits of pythons, the dubious benefits or otherwise of having one living in his property, and the numerous experiences of his younger days when he lived in the wilds of Africa.

I was amazed, and not a little horrified, that he agreed to take on this reptile. We, or rather I, had to do the property inspections and check-in, the staff refusing to go anywhere near the property whilst the snake was in residence. I always made sure this tenant was present in the house when I carried out the inspections. The python was eleven feet long and lived in a massive tank in the living room. Apparently it was quite harmless and he regularly took it down to the local pub, wrapped around his shoulders, to entertain the locals. He never took it out of the tank when I was present… Thank God!

Arachnides

On a different occasion, I arrived at a property to carry out an inspection only to find that the tenant, a nurse, had a much smaller tank, this time housing a tarantula. She had not asked permission for this pet, and I could not decide whether it constituted a pet in the sense implied by the tenancy clause banning animals in the properties. In the case of spiders, how could they cause any damage?

This tenant offered to take her pet tarantula out of its tank and put it in my hands. I always assumed tarantulas were poisonous creatures but she assured me the biggest danger with anyone holding a tarantula is to the tarantula itself. If it is dropped it would splat. I began to think differently about harm to the property, especially to the carpets, if the tarantula was ever in the hands of someone a little nervous like me. In fact, I was exceedingly nervous, disliking spiders at the best of times, let alone large hairy ones the size of a small saucer - so I declined.

Canis familiaris

The reason why the 'no-pets' clause is included in tenancy agreements is because of potential damage by soiling, the scratching of doors and furniture, and chewing, to name but a few of the misdemeanours of supposedly domesticated animals. The landlord can, of course, override the clause. We had many rural, and often isolated, properties that would have been difficult to let had the landlords not allowed dogs to accompany the tenants for their security.

There was one gentleman farmer on our books whose ancestors were presumably the historic Lords of the Manor (in which he lived). He owned the best part of a village on the edge of the Acle marshes and we managed a quantity of the estate cottages for him. A great animal lover himself, he was prepared to allow dogs into his properties but with one proviso. The tenants had to understand that if he, the landlord, found any dog worrying his sheep, he would shoot first and concern for his tenants and their dog would be secondary.

Lost and Found

The property that had housed the tarantula and its tenant owner was eventually the source of further interesting revelations. During the whole time I ran my business I only ever had one policeman in my properties - the victim of a marital breakdown.

On the day this policeman moved into the property, recently vacated by our arachnid-loving tenant, his first experience was to have the trailer with his possessions stolen from outside the property. A month or so later, he rang me and began asking me various questions about the property, and the cooker in particular; where had it come from, who owned it, who owned the property, who had lived there...? I was rather mystified, and eventually asked, was there a problem? My thoughts were that maybe the cooker was in a dangerous state, or it had been a stolen item. "Yes, there is a problem," he said, "I have the Drug Squad here."

It transpired that this policeman had dropped his car keys down the back of the cooker which stood by the back door, and, in trying to fish them out, he had hooked up a sizable packet of cannabis instead. I was able to provide the Officers the forwarding address of the tenant who had just vacated the property. She a had a boyfriend who visited regularly, and there had always been a noticeable number of rather dubious-looking characters milling in and out of the property when we attended for inspections. I can only assume that someone had been caught short and hid the packet behind the cooker (which happened to be situated right next to the back door) whilst making a quick exit.

More strange inhabitants

Even more unnerving was the number of properties sporting the more ethereal type of inhabitant. Norfolk is renowned for the number of haunted buildings and my portfolio was not short of them. The problem was that once we received confirmation of these ethereal residents I felt duty-bound to inform potential tenants. Most presences are completely benign, but many people are very uncomfortable with the unknown.

On a couple of occasions, I attended a potential take-on where the landlords admitted to their invisible, but oft-evident resident. I would advise them that there were ways and means of clearing the house of any such disturbances but often they did not want the presences removed! I explained that I could not justifiably let a property knowing it was haunted without advising potential tenants. At least two properties did not come my way because of this advice.

One of the first properties I had taken on was on its second let when my colleague returned from carrying out a check-out inspection after the tenants had left. She complained that it had felt very eerie, especially upstairs. I told her it was probably the wind whistling through the eves or the TV aerial - it was a dormer bungalow.

Some while later, having just carried out an inspection at this same property, I was having coffee with the new tenant when she told me some surprising facts. Did I know the property was haunted? I said I didn't, but I was not surprised, and explained about my colleague's experience. "Yes, it's a female," she said "you mostly hear her walking to-and-fro across the landing." She then proceeded to tell me that, often, when vacuuming upstairs, the plug would come out of the socket. "She doesn't seem to like other women being in the house."

I explained that if she was unhappy with this presence we could try and find her another property. "Oh, it's a minor inconvenience, I don't mind – I'm quite sensitive to picking up paranormal phenomena. The ghost is the landlord's wife – I let him come in and talk to her." Apparently the landlord's wife had died of a massive heart attack in the downstairs bedroom. The activity upstairs was seemingly due to the fact that, at one time, their son had been very sick and she had paced the landing outside his bedroom.

Experts in the field say that paranormal activity in property results from periods of high emotion during a deceased previous occupant's life being absorbed by the fabric. Certain people with particular brain wave activity are able to tune in and pick up these signals which is why some people are conscious of ghostly activity and others, with different brain waves, are not. The best description of these phenomena is that walls become like the tape in an old fashioned recorder and at periods of high emotion the walls absorb the activity and record it. ("The Mask of Time" by Joan Foreman)

This tenant, with her highly attuned brainwaves, remained for quite a while in the property. After she left, the landlord, who had meanwhile found himself a new partner, decided to sell the property.

COMPETITION & COUNSELLING

Poachers

In the earlier days of my business I was showing some applicants around the rather grand residence of Bacton Hall, situated near the North Norfolk coast, not too far distant from the terminal where the pipelines from the rigs that extract the oil from the bed of the North Sea deposit it for storage and onward distribution. The applicants were accompanied by their Surveyor – in fact it was the Surveyor who had arranged the appointment on behalf of his clients. We had quite a few insurance case applicants where damage had been caused

134

to their homes, either through subsidence, fire, or other disaster, therefore they required temporary accommodation whilst repairs were undertaken.

On this occasion, we had concluded the viewing, having discussed the terms of the letting in the comfortable living room. As the applicants were taking a final wander around the property they were expecting would become their home for the foreseeable future, the surveyor and I got chatting. He was intrigued by my business, no doubt because I was a sole trader woman – still a rarity in those days of the early 'nineties.

Being somewhat proud of my achievement to date, I was happy to tell this Surveyor how I had started my business, and my philosophy regarding it, but I gradually got the impression I was being probed about the nature of the business for other reasons. I did not realise at the time that he had a brother who ran an estate agency in Norwich. It was not too long afterwards that I discovered the Surveyor had added a lettings department to his surveying business, no doubt working comfortably in liaison with his estate agent brother.

Increasing Competition

That signalled the beginning of competition. By the mid-1990s many new letting agents began springing up as entrepreneurs realised the potential of the 1988 Housing Act. Estate agents, too, began opening letting departments as housing sales flattened with the worsening economy. When properties would not sell, the obvious way forward in their minds, was to persuade their clients to rent out their properties until the housing market picked up, especially once the building societies came to understand more fully the new rules brought in by the 1988 Act and relaxed their once-stringent stipulations.

The idea of converting properties designated for sale into lets was so that homeowners would receive an income to fund the cost of their

135

next abode, also to have the properties inhabited for security reasons rather than have them lying empty and vulnerable. The advantage to the agent was that they would have the benefit of holding on to the properties, gaining the rental commission meantime, until the market improved for the selling thereof.

Dual Agencies

In some cases, we were offered property to let that was for sale with an estate agent that had no lettings department. Owners were hedging their bets – they would go with whatever occurred first, a let or sale. I always advised clients this was not a good idea, much as I would have liked the additional properties to add to my portfolio. With a joint agency, each party - selling or letting - tended not to pay as much attention to marketing these properties as one would with a sole-agency property. For example, when choosing each week which properties to feature in advertisements, one naturally chose those that were the most likely to speedily bring in an income.

Many were the times when the owner ignored our advice and insisted we should take on their property regardless. We would eventually find a prospective tenant and ring the owner to let them know of our success, only to be told: "Oh what a pity! I've only just accepted an offer for its sale!". We had wasted our time and money promoting the property and attending for viewings – and caused annoyance and inconvenience to the prospective tenants who were banking on the property for their future, albeit temporary, home.

The Stress Categories

Life has a strange way of sorting out one's ambitions, as I had already experienced with my first career. Did I regret not having the opportunity to become a Counsellor which had been the original career intention of my more mature years?

Besides caring for the properties under our management, we found ourselves being a sounding board for the woes of our prospective tenants – and sometimes even landlords. There were various categories of landlords and tenants. Because the new Housing Act, many people were starting to rent out of choice – because of temporary job positions, or testing out a new area before purchasing, etc. These people often became landlords themselves as they left behind their original homes either because they were on temporary job secondments, or the market was such that they were unable to sell.

Also, property inheritance was entering a new phase of being not merely the privilege of the aristocratic classes. We had prospective landlords who had just lost a parent or favourite relative who had bequeathed them their home. Sentimental attachment made it difficult for them to envisage selling. Renting out these properties, therefore, was a route they often chose in order to make some benefit from their inheritance until such time as their feelings of attachment to the property became more distant. Often these clients were in a stressed or emotional state.

In the case of tenants, they were mostly in the situation of needing property because of some unfortunate occurrence in their lives. Some had never got beyond being on hard times financially, and often pent-up resentment would flare up as a consequence. Others had more recently fallen into such difficulty and had lost their homes because of job loss, or because the mortgage interest rates had increased or they had over-mortgaged themselves (or both), with the consequence that their homes had been repossessed.

Very many were from broken marriages, either with no family and were lonely, or, more sadly, men who had left young families behind, not necessarily because they had wanted to leave the family home, but because life with the wife had become intolerable, or she had abandoned him for a new partner. These latter renters had a double-whammy of top stress factors. Often, as they came in to complete some aspect of their application, out would come not only their pen or deposit, but also the anger and vitriol they had bottled up which the bruising reality of what they were about to embark upon, highlighted.

Post-Christmas was often a busy time for us. Clients would come in, having fallen out with their spouse or partner during the enforced, and often claustrophobic, time spent together during this winter holiday period. We would sort out accommodation for them, only to find that, a few days before they were due to move in, they would no longer need the rental property because they had kissed and made up!

The Single Parent

Occasionally we would have a woman with a child or children in tow who would be seeking a roof over their heads. This was often problematic because they were mothers of school-aged, or even pre-school children, and they had no, or, at best, poorly paid, part-time jobs. Sometimes a parent, or even a guilty 'ex', would act as guarantor, only for the latter having second thoughts and changing their mind at the last minute, or some six months or so down the line. Or they could find no suitable guarantor at all.

We were very aware that these various categories of house movers, be they landlords or tenants, felt pressured. It is said that house-moving is among the top three most stressful occurrences in life – the others being death of a loved one, and marital break-up. Some of the clients seeking our services had the burden of experiencing two of these factors. These various applicants would pour out their hearts to us and the counsellor in me would let them do so. We would offer them what words of comfort we could, and even a cup of tea. We eventually found ourselves, 'entre nous', referring to the business as

'Heron Property Management and Counselling Services Ltd'. All in all, it was a very rewarding occupation.

Spring in the Air

I remember a young girl in such a position applying to rent a property. She had three very young children and, for some months, they had been living in bed-and-breakfast accommodation provided by the Council as a temporary measure. Not only had she left a violent husband, but trying to cope with three young children in such accommodation was almost beyond her. She could not afford much, and I knew from previous such cases that the process of getting her established in a let property would not be simple. She would need a guarantor as she was not in work.

We found her an old farmhouse that did not have the best form of heating, and was not in a brilliant state of décor, but it was the cheapest and most suitable for her needs. She loved it. Her father was prepared to act as guarantor and all seemed to be progressing well. It turned out her father had an historic County Court judgement against him and the landlord's legal protection insurance would have been rendered invalid had we accepted him as guarantor. Naturally the tears flowed from this stoic young lady when we broke the news to her. Council house waiting lists meant she could be in her temporary accommodation for many more months. The young children needed a settled environment especially after the trauma they had experienced. I was desperate to try and help her.

She went away hoping to find someone else who was prepared to fulfil the role of guarantor for her. Meanwhile, in fairness to the landlord, we could not hold the property, particularly as it seemed she would have difficulty finding the means for renting it. After a second false start, and more tears, she eventually came back with a guarantor who was a very sympathetic neighbour of her Father who obviously knew her well from childhood. The property, as it happened, was still available, and all finally went through successfully.

It was springtime by the time she could move in, and the poor heating would not have too much of a detrimental effect – she would have time to improve things before the onset of next winter. She was elated, and we shared her happiness. It befell me to check her in to the property on a Saturday morning. There was a wilderness of a garden for the children to play in and they gambolled about freely as we conducted the business arrangements indoors. She came out to wave me off. As I was driving away, I caught sight of her in my wing mirror, leaping high into the air for joy. I felt a lump in my throat - and even now, today as I write this, it brings tears to my eyes. For me, too, I was so happy to be doing this work – fulfilling in so many ways.

~

REFLECTION:

CARING & TRUSTING

The good Lord made us in his own image and likeness (Gen 1:26). Who are we, then, to treat each other differently; dependant on status, appearance, income, or sinfulness? Jesus welcomes us all equally, Jew or Gentile, saint or sinner, and urges that we should do likewise by treating our neighbour as we would wish to be treated ourselves (Matt 7:12). This was the 'mission statement' upon which I wished my business to run, but there were the occasional pitfalls.

Caring implies an element of trust. We trust that the people we care for will not stab us in the back. A selfless caring can involve risk, so our trusting needs to be tempered with wisdom that comes from the Lord's guidance through His Holy Spirit. Does that mean, when a judgement we make is misplaced, we have been misguided? Maybe it is because we have trusted unwisely. In making a judgement we may have trusted in our own strength rather than the Lord's. People who are given great trust can often be swayed by worldly rewards - as, of course, can all of God's creatures, not merely those laden with trust.

When the Lord chose those who were to follow Him to help Him with His mission, He selected twelve whom He trusted would be behind Him. He had exhorted Judas, along with the other eleven, to go out and "heal the sick, raise the dead, cleanse those who have leprosy, drive out demons" Matt (10:8). But human frailty caused Judas to betray Him. Was the Lord's trust misplaced? When He chose Judas to be one of the twelve, Jesus knew that he was the one who would betray Him (John 6:64). As one of the twelve, He would have cared for him regardless and must have seen the good in him initially.

Sometimes, when our trust is misplaced, maybe we are being put on the spot so that we don't become big-headed about our own abilities – it is a reminder, a lesson, perhaps – that when our judgements go wrong, we should have been a little more immersed in prayer for guidance and not clouded by our own preconceptions. Those of us doing the trusting may not always notice subtle changes in those who are the beneficiaries of that trust and we end up being metaphorically 'stabbed in the back'. At the end of the day, with the frailty of human nature, and given the gift of free will, the choice to follow Jesus or deny Him, can be changed at a whim.

THOUGHTS FOR DISCUSSION

1. How often do we make wrong judgements, maybe because we assess people based on our own inherent prejudices?

2. As we mature, we come to realise that people often have very different experiences to ourselves, therefore they think differently and as a result often appear to have strange foibles or ideas. How open are you to accepting people where they are at?

3. Is it good to trust, and what are the repercussions if we do? And if we don't?

--ooOoo--

Chapter 8

UNDER THE CLOUD

COLD COMFORT

Back History

I had laboured with pain and discomfort in my spine for over 30 years. It peaked and troughed according to how I used it - or abused it, as I was eventually to learn when finally taught how to live within its capabilities.

My philosophy in life had been to put every ounce of mental and/or physical energy into everything I did, not only into my sporting activities when a teenager. My physical problem was gradually worsening with passing years as the condition seemed to be travelling upwards along the spine.

I had always assumed it was there for life and one just had to get on with it. At age 15, I was diagnosed as having a disc that kept slipping, and subsequently a sacroiliac joint problem. Over time, I underwent a manipulation under anaesthetic, received occasional bouts of physiotherapy, and was given special corsets to wear for support. After the experience in Israel, and a subsequent visit to the Doctor, the physiotherapist I was referred to told me that, unless I did some exercise (difficult during my marriage and child-rearing years), my back would seize up altogether.

All Going Swimmingly

I started swimming. The girls were still at home at this time and invariably I drove a car full of teenagers to a sports club at Filby - a lovely ride out into the country, and very therapeutic after a day's work. One of my daughters' friends even taught me how to dive. It was a wonderful feeling of release to have the freedom and support of the water around one's aching body, to be followed by the soothing heat of the sauna.

We had great fun. The Club was frequented by the lads from RAF Coltishall and there were times when we managed to squeeze twenty-five of us into a rather small sauna. The jokes and ribaldry were a delight to me, not to mention to my daughters and their friends.

A Paddle

A year or two later, as the disability became worse, I found the bending involved in putting on footwear very difficult. One of the catalogue firms sold clogs made from sheepskin, and I found wearing these in winter negated the problem of donning socks and shoes. As a family, we loved beach walking, and many a Christmas and/or New Year's Day was spent in this pastime.

On this particular New Year's Day, I headed off to the beach with a car full of my teenagers and some of their friends. I sat in the car overlooking the sea as I watched ruefully as they went off for their walk. I was feeling very negative about the fact that I was unable to join them, but I could at least savour the sea air through the open car window.

As I sat there mulling over the disadvantages of my condition, and feeling generally miserable, I suddenly had an idea. I could at least walk the short distance with my sticks to the water's edge and properly savour the seaside experience. Once there, I had the irrational desire to paddle – it was a freezing cold day. I kicked off my mules, hitched up my trousers from the knees, and entered the freezing water. The water was icy cold and my feet glowed, but very pleasantly so. The exhilaration was indescribable. Above all, I was overcome by the most incredible sense of achievement. I was doing something that most people couldn't, or, more realistically, wouldn't do – and I was ability impaired. My mood changed dramatically.

The New Year's Day paddle has since become a tradition whenever I am in Norfolk for the celebration. Family members, or friends, around for the holiday, are usually willing to come for the walk, but few are mad enough to be encouraged to join me in the sea.

MEDICAL MATTERS

Medical Intervention?

I was meeting some prospective tenants one day and made my exit from the car in my increasingly struggling fashion. Even walking was by now proving more and more difficult. As the tour of the property they were viewing concluded, it became apparent that my movements had been acutely observed by the female of the party who turned out to be an osteopath. She seemed to think I should not be out and about, but at home resting, and advised that I should seek serious help for my problem.

My GP referred me back to the Practice Physio who worked on me for a few weeks before sending me off to the Physiotherapy Department at the Norfolk & Norwich Hospital. I was placed under the care of the Senior Physiotherapist who spent another three months trying, by various means, to get my spine sorted, including using acupuncture. I was most surprised to learn that what I had previously considered to be only a complementary medical practice, had been used by the NHS for over 25 years. This Physio was also unable to make an impression on my condition, and finally she referred me to the Pain Clinic.

At the Pain Clinic, I was placed in front of a group that comprised six Consultants in the fields of gynaecology, rheumatology, orthopaedics, psychiatry, neurology, and another whose field of specialism I remember not what. I was questioned and put through my paces – this was after having to accept help from one of these senior clinicians to remove my boots as I could not even bend properly to do this myself. Finally, I was sent for a CAT scan which proved inconclusive, so an appointment was made for me to see the orthopaedic surgeon.

Mr No-Bedside-Manner

My first encounter with the renowned Mr Tucker, the senior Orthopaedic Consultant, was interesting. Before meeting him face-to-face, I heard him outside the cubicle in which I had been placed to await his examination, giving one of his minions a dressing down for operating some equipment over the weekend which he apparently considered an unnecessary expenditure. He obviously held some major role in the management of the hospital finances. He sounded quite intimidating.

Argument over, he came in, and I was surprised to see a diminutive character, quite bent with a scoliosis of the spine. I learnt, somewhat later, that he did not trust his colleagues to operate on him to rectify his problem, even though he himself performed such operations, as he had done on the 12-year-old daughter of a friend of mine.

With no preamble, I was asked how, on a scale of one to ten, I considered my pain. Rather nervously, I first had to ask him whether 'ten' was top or bottom (my reverse logic again?) Once we established that ten indicated a high level of pain, I then had to ask him: "Compared to what?" I had suffered pain for most of my life and could not remember what it was like to be pain-free. I forget the answer I finally gave him, but he had already deduced that an MRI scan was necessary before he could complete the diagnosis. This gave me hope that maybe an operation would be possible after all, and freedom from this debilitating pain could be in sight.

The Modern Machine

MRI machines were still a relatively new invention in 1993, and our local NHS hospital, the Norfolk & Norwich, did not own one. The NHS had to buy time to use the one owned by the local BUPA private hospital. Mr Tucker asked me if I could pay the £500 it would cost to put me through this machine. I pointed out that I had only recently commenced my own business and had not long come off State Benefits, and I had no savings.

An MRI scan is not a pleasant experience, especially if one is claustrophobic. It is also not a good experience for anyone who has to keep moving to gain a modicum of relief from their pain. A spinal scan lasts approximately 20-25 minutes, and one must remain completely still throughout, or they must start the process again from the beginning.

Once over, I began to think of the outcome. Did I truly want to know? If the diagnosis resulted in an operation, the diagnosis would be a good outcome. I might even be able to resume playing tennis and squash – sports I had been so keen on in my earlier days. If not, I would be saddled with this disabling pain for the rest of my life. I got to the point where I did not want to know the answer – because, for as long as I did not know, I had hope.

Three months went by and I heard nothing regarding the results. I was living on the edge of my nerves as I discovered one day when I broke down over the most minor of procedures at the local Health

147

Centre. The nurse extracted from me the root of my concerns, and within a few days I had an appointment to attend the Hospital.

The Wreck

The day arrived and I went to the hospital accompanied by a 'friend' who seemed convinced I was making a fuss over nothing. I hoped she was right. My turn eventually arrived, and Mr Tucker did not mince his words. "Your back is a wreck – there is nothing we can do. Come and see the pictures." To this day, I cannot bear to think of the images that were supposed to be my spine. That was the sum of his interest in me as far as the consultation was concerned, and probably why the Hospital had not even bothered to contact me, as there was nothing they could do – why waste an appointment?

I needed time to digest this outcome, and was desperate to go for a chat over a cup of coffee. I was taken by my companion to a coffee machine and had to stand there to drink it. I took as long as possible over my drink, and was hustled away as soon as I had finished as my 'friend' said she wanted to get home. She seemed somewhat disappointed that the outcome was not what she had expected. What I desperately needed was a chat, just to talk things out of my system, and maybe receive some words of comfort or encouragement – I was not really bothered about the coffee. We parted company, and I did not know where to go as I could not face returning to the office.

WHAT CAN BE DONE?

Despair

I drove around all afternoon not knowing what to do with myself. Eventually I returned to Brundall at the end of the working day only to find that all my close friends happened to be out. Finally, I drove to our parish church, being quite unsure whether it would be open.

After all, was that not where people go in times of great distress? Maybe a heart-to-heart with God might straighten me out somewhat, and help me to see things more rationally.

Surprisingly, the church was open. There happened to be an end-of-year Mass for the teachers of the local Catholic schools that was just finishing. I wanted to avoid people but, having got this far, I did not feel like turning away. Hesitantly, I crept into the back of the church hoping not to be noticed. I suppose it was inevitable that I would be discovered. The next thing I knew, I was in front of the Blessed Sacrament Chapel being comforted by a teacher whom I knew by sight, but did not know well at all. She spent almost three hours with me, talking and praying, and missing the party she should have attended following the Mass.

I shall never forget her kindness and selflessness, and her words of encouragement. They were not platitudes, but in my state at the time, I could not believe all she was saying. In retrospect, of course, she was so right. One thing that did register with me of what she said, was that one day I would be able to help others who may be going through similar experiences. I could not see it at the time.

Prayer Group

During the course of evening she mentioned the Prayer Group held at the Church and suggested I came along. For years I had desperately longed to have a deeper involvement with my Faith rather than just the mere attendance at Sunday Mass. Being the product of a mixed marriage, having had a mixed marriage of my own, and supporting my husband's endeavours alongside bringing up the children, there had been little time or opportunity for additional involvement.

I had been very much used to an ecumenical environment. My convent boarding school comprised at least a third of pupils who were not Catholic, and half of my siblings had turned to the more active evangelical-style of church and, anyway, lived some distance away, so little support from them either. I had seen mention of the Renewal Prayer Group in the Parish Newsletter and longed to find out more, but had not had the courage to go along on my own. Now I had a contact.

Depression

Following the diagnosis there were some months of serious depression. I eventually learnt that most people with my spinal condition end up virtually bedridden, and I have been told on more than one occasion I could even become completely paralysed. I was devastated. I could not see any point being on earth any longer, suffering increasing pain and debility – I simply wanted to be with Jesus. One's thinking can get greatly distorted when the mind is distressed. I became very suicidal for the second time in my life. This time it somehow felt more dangerous as the children were no longer fully dependent on me.

However, I did start attending the Prayer Group. The first few visits I can only describe as strange. Each time I sat near the back, thinking that if I did not like what was going on, at any point I could sneak away, but each week I was drawn back for more. So why did I go? Was it the lovely people who were so open and friendly? Or maybe it was some way of trying to get back that closeness to God that I had experienced in my late teens/early twenties? God seemed very distant to me at this time and I was not very happy with Him to say the least – in fact, I was decidedly angry with Him.

Thy Will be Done

Some time later, I remember speaking to our Parish Priest about my anger with God. He seemed to think it was a healthy sign, as it showed I still had a relationship with Him. Some years even later, I woke up one morning with the strong realisation that, if I was angry with God, I was actually putting myself in God's place. In reality, I was telling God what was best for me, rather than allowing His will to be done. A very humbling thought.

AN EXCEPTIONAL BLESSING

Assisi

On the trip to the Holy Land the previous year, I had met a lovely girl from the neighbouring parish of North Walsham who suggested I joined their pilgrimage to Assisi and Rome scheduled for the following year. This was due to commence six weeks following my diagnosis.

My condition had worsened gradually over thirty years or so, so I was not expecting any immediate drastic deterioration that would hamper my ability to join the pilgrimage. Nevertheless, I thought it prudent to mention the diagnosis to the priest who was running the pilgrimage so that he was aware of what he was taking on. "No problem at all," says he, "Of course you can still come. We always take a wheelchair anyway". I hastily assured him my condition had not got to that stage and I was quite capable of walking. At that time my main complaint, aside from some reasonably manageable pain, seemed to be this bad bout of depression. So off we went.

There were a few blissfully peaceful days spent in the beautiful countryside of Assisi, in the Region of Umbria. Assisi was the home of St Francis, one of my favourite saints – the first known ecologist, a lover of nature and of peace, and with a passion for Christ. After exploring the Saint's haunts, we then had to leave for the hustle and bustle of Rome which I expected to be a little more hectic and physically challenging.

Racing for Rome

The initial challenge, however, was rather more exceptional than expected. We were told to be up by 5am, breakfasted by 5.30 and ready to depart at 6am for the 3.5-hour journey to Rome for our first destination, a fixed-time appointment at 11am - an audience with the Pope. The problem was twofold; firstly we needed to be there by 10am in order to get decent seats in the Audience Hall; secondly, our means of transport for getting there, our pilgrimage coach - had vanished overnight!

We had a furious pilgrimage leader in our midst – one could almost witness the steam coming from his cranial orifices. We were encouraged to pray for the situation whilst he made frantic phone calls to the coach company. After some while, another coach was sourced and we were able to commence our journey to Rome - by this time over an hour later than scheduled.

The road from Assisi to Rome was not a good one, with many potholes, causing us to bounce around in our seats – I trust it has improved somewhat since. What is more, we were racing down at speed which did not do my poor spine any good at all. As we approached the parking for our destination, (by this time it was 10.35) our leader barked out the orders for disembarking the coach. "Once you are off – run! Anne, you get in the wheelchair, and Claire, you push!" I would have done anything to have run with the others, or at least fast-walked, to loosen up my spine as I had sat long enough through a very painful journey, but there was no time to argue. I did as I was told.

The Papal Audience

If the coach ride from Assisi was bad for those with poor spines, the bumping over Rome's cobbled streets in a wheelchair was torture to say the least. We finally arrived to join the queue at the door to the

Hall, and I made to vacate the chair no longer required, aiming for a bit of relief and a good stretch. "Wheelchairs down to the next door" called out an orderly. "But I no longer need to be in it!" I protested. Our leader advised I should stay put, and I was wheeled down to the next door and into the front of the hall.

To my dismay, there were three long rows of wheelchair-users with their companion-pushers, and I and my companion had to sit amongst them. I was mortified. I had never been in a wheelchair before. I was desperate to be with the rest of the gang. I managed to turn enough to see a massive, packed hall, so vast we were unable to see the remainder of our party which must have been right at the back. Even being two rows from the front, the Pope - John Paul II - when he made his entry, still seemed to be quite a distance away.

At the end of the audience, the Pope descended the stage and started moving towards the wheelchairs. To my surprise, he came amongst all the 'sick' (as we were labelled) and blessed each one of us individually. I was so uncomfortable with my spurious situation, coupled with my depression, that the significance of this encounter did not fully register with me at the time. When we eventually met up with the rest of the party they were very excited on my behalf. On my return, my Mother, when she heard what had happened, was overjoyed. As for me, I even had to be persuaded to pick up the photos of the event.

Care and Compassion

It was not all doom and gloom. My fellow pilgrims became great friends. The unobtrusive care and compassion, and the prayerful support I received from them, were great blessings and I learnt to become more accepting of my condition. I even began to appreciate the increased comfort of sitting in the said wheelchair instead of the seats and chairs that were provided at the different venues we visited.

I shared its use with another of the party who had injured her ankle on the trip – she needed it for when we were on the move, and because it was present and available in between her need for it, I was encouraged to take it over. I must say I did begin to appreciate the comfort it afforded over the hard, armless chairs.

At the airport on the return home, I was persuaded to sit in the wheelchair rather than have someone push it around empty. I found it a great comfort not to have to stand in the queues. The girls enjoyed the opportunity of pushing the wheelchair, so I was persuaded to stay in it so they could all have a turn. Even more so, after they had purchased their Duty Free goods, they all wanted a turn at pushing so that they could off-load their goods on to me so that I became almost buried by their bags and bottles. We had quite some fun passing through Marco Polo Airport with me as their mobilised packhorse.

On my return home, the depression had not much abated. Yet some days I would feel more uplifted than others. My fellow pilgrims had been most supportive and understanding whilst I was among them, and this continued on my return. I would often receive a phone call from one or other, which seemed to coincide with days when my spirits had been raised. During the conversation, I was frequently told "We prayed for you at Mass this morning." This is when I first began to truly believe in the power of prayer.

DETERIORATION

Miracles do happen

On my return, I continued to attend the Prayer Group, still receiving, rather than being in any position to be giving in my prayer. Days of Renewal are arranged by the Prayer Group on a couple of occasions a year when we have a speaker for the day.

On this, my first experience of a Renewal Day, it was Sister Josephine Walsh who was our guest speaker. Sr. Josephine is renowned for having a great gift of healing. At the end of her talk she invited anyone who wished to come up to receive healing prayer. I felt duty-bound to do my best for my condition so, somewhat sceptically, I went up and asked for healing for my spine – she prayed over me but, pretty much as I expected, nothing happened.

At our Prayer Group meeting the following week, there was a lot of enthusiasm about the previous Saturday's Renewal Day, and people spoke of the many blessings they had received. We all related our experiences in turn. When it came to me, I was asked what I thought about the day. I remember thinking that I couldn't share the undoubted enthusiasm of the rest of the group, and I said so. I was asked; "Why do you think that is?" I replied that maybe it was because I had joined the day halfway through because I was at work until midday on Saturdays. Then, for one who, at the time, was still most extremely shy, the most incredible thing happened.

I barely knew the members of this group, having only recently joined, and I had been brought up to have a very stiff upper lip. Regardless, I found myself bursting into loud, uncontrollable sobbing, and in words I could not recognise as my own, I burbled out all this stuff about feeling suicidal. The truth was that I had felt very suicidal since the diagnosis. The children had become pretty much independent, so the responsibility I had felt towards them, when previously experiencing such thoughts after my marriage broke up, was no longer a restraining hand. On the contrary, with the prognosis I had been given, I felt, instead, that I would eventually become a burden to them. They would be better off without me.

However, there was a Restraining Hand at work on this occasion, too. I was sharing transport to a swimming club with a friend whose work colleague for whom she was directly responsible, had recently committed suicide. The devastation this friend experienced because of her work colleague's actions, made me realise I could not repeat the same for her to encounter a second time. If my companion swimmer was to experience a second death by a similar cause, it would be totally unbearable for her. The feelings of wanting to finish my life did not disappear, despite knowing I could not carry out the 'want' because of this friend. I am not sure I would have been brave enough to do so anyway.

One could say that what I experienced was beyond belief. After my extraordinary outpouring at Prayer Group, I have not, from that day to this, ever again harboured a further suicidal thought, even though the depression lingered and the condition worsened. The Lord, in His love, knew what was more important for me at that time. The healing prayer I had received on the Renewal Day had a delayed result, but not the one I expected - my damaged thinking was obviously deemed a more important candidate for healing than my damaged spine. Often, we don't always get what we pray for – we should trust the Lord knows best what is right for us. Also, we don't always get an answer to prayer when we expect it, which is usually straight away, but it comes in God's own time.

Getting it in the Neck

The depression continued but no longer encompassing the suicidal tendencies, despite further traumas to come. Some weeks after the visit to Rome, and the experience at the Prayer Group, I woke up one morning with the most excruciating pain around the back and base of my head and I could not lift my head off the pillow. It was a terrifying experience. Somebody called the Medical Centre but there was no way I could drive there, or even be driven, to see the Doctor. The Duty Doctor came to the house around midday by which time the pain had eased a little and I had managed to get out of bed and was organising the essentials of running my business. This made him rather cross as he said I should have been resting.

I eventually got to see my own Doctor, who could say nothing more than this was an extension of the same problem. He sent me for an x-ray. I asked the radiographer what she had found, but professionally she was not allowed to say. She did, however, advise that if I had a neck collar I should wear it, and to go to the doctor as soon as possible for the results. I found this rather scary.

Diagnostics and Help

The neck collar soon turned into a neck brace that I was advised to wear for half an hour at a time, with a break in between. I learnt that this was in order that the brace did not take over completely the support of the head by weakening the neck muscles too much.

The depression did not improve. Eventually my Mother stepped into the breach and suggested I should see her private Consultant in Nottingham, Mr Mulholland, who happened to be a Professor of Orthopaedics.

The consultation with him resulted in the best information I had received to date regarding my condition. He explained that the discs between the vertebrae had lost their water and had dried out so that they showed up black on the scan – sometimes referred to as black disc disease within the medical profession. Effectively, this meant there was no cushioning between the vertebrae, thereby causing the pain. He told me that the fact I had had to keep going, bringing up the children on my own, had proved beneficial. He added that most people with the condition become virtually bedridden.

Mr Mulholland went on to explain that an operation was possible when the vertebrae could be hinged, but he did not recommend it as my musculature was in a relatively good state which he associated with the aforementioned need to keep going, bringing up the children as a sole parent. Any benefit I would gain in skeletal strength resulting from such an operation would be lost in a weakened musculature. He would write to my Consultant at the Norfolk & Norwich Hospital with his findings.

I asked this Consultant if, had I come to him earlier, some remedial or preventive action might have been possible. He explained that they might have been deceived into operating, only to find that the discs above and below would eventually collapse also. He further added that there was a congenital element to the condition - it was not due to normal degeneration.

What he did not tell me at the time was that because of the lack of proper disc protection between the vertebrae, some of these latter had already become damaged and I would likely experience future vertebral damage, with the possible consequence of nerve impairment which could lead to paralysis – the cervical neck area being the most dangerous part of the skeleton for this to happen.

Palliative Care

On my return to Norfolk I was transferred out of Mr Tucker's domain in Orthopaedics and sent to the Rheumatology Department instead. Palliative care was implemented and a wheelchair to support me when sitting – I was still trying to keep my business going but desk work was by no means a comfortable experience.

When the wheelchair was delivered the despair about my future truly set in. It was a gross contraption. Although it had wheels, its use was intended more as a static chair - the sort of thing you find in the communal lounges of care homes for old people, more often than not inhabited by sleep-ridden seniors not too far away from being carried out in a final pain-free, prone position. There was no way this could be transported in a car.

Because I worked from home, lived on my own, and bearing in mind my gregarious nature, a social life outside of the confines of home and office was very important to me. I played Bridge, I attended Prayer Group and Mass; I had meals, coffee mornings, and Book Club meetings at friends' homes, etc. Up until now, I had often used a folding high-backed garden chair to support my spine which was easily transportable. This was deemed no longer safe or suitable.

I could not see how I was to continue to mix socially with such a monstrosity of a wheelchair, nor would I wish to be seen in it publicly. Yet I was far from ready to become a stay-at-home cripple. Tears of sheer frustration followed and flowed.

Problem Solving

It was not too long before a solution was found. If the chair could not be transported inside a car, then there would have to be another way. It involved a tow bar being fitted to the rear of my car – not for a trailer, but for a bike rack-like attachment onto which the folded wheelchair could be supported and secured.

Everyone got to know when I was out and about as my car became an icon with its gross appendage on the back. I had to swallow my pride if I wanted to continue living something of a social life. It was bad enough going about with a neck brace – what matter another humiliation?

Because I could still walk, a little at least – and needed to, I referred to my chair as a chair on wheels, not a wheelchair. Sitting too long was not comfortable, neither was walking for too long, and standing was even worse. I had to constantly keep moving my position to gain a modicum of relief. Different sections of the spine seemed to benefit from certain positions, support, or movements, but it was hard to find a method or position that was comfortable for the whole of the spine at any one time.

Sorry State

It took me four years before I felt comfortable going out and about with my unusual condition and its essential accoutrements. I often wished I had some normal, recognisable condition that people could understand. In appearance I looked perfectly healthy – my GP was frequently telling me my looks belied what was going on beneath the surface.

I knew no one else in a similar medical state. If there was anybody around so afflicted then maybe they were the stay-at-home cripples, or already bed-ridden as the Consultant had predicted was possible, or maybe too embarrassed even to attempt venturing out. I often felt very sorry for myself. People would tell me that there were other people worse off, but that is precious little consolation when you are in the midst of your own suffering and resultant depression.

TURNING POINTS

The Head Case

My turning point came when attending a party locally. I had heard of this young mother who had suffered cancer over the years and it had now reached her spine. What surprised me greatly was that she was attending the party with her head supported by a cage made from spindles, nuts, and bolts. The cancer had reached her neck and it could not support her head at all.

It was a huge wake-up call for me. Who was I to complain? I may have a very uncomfortable future ahead, but at least I had a future, even should I become bedridden or paralysed. This young mum's cancer was terminal. She was ten years younger than me and she had four children whose ages at the time ranged from eight to eighteen. She would not even see her children fully grown up, let alone any grandchildren. If she was brave enough to support such a construction in public, then my embarrassments were minimal by comparison.

I had never seen anyone wearing this type of medical contraption. At least my brace would have been witnessed being worn by serious accident victims, or as often seen used in the TV episodes of "Casualty" and other medical-type screenings. I do not know if this unfortunate fellow villager ever got to learn of the huge impact she effected upon my life. I never had the courage or the opportunity to tell her as it was not long after the party when she died. My depression gradually lifted and I got on with running my life - and my business - with the full attention they both deserved.

Example

The encounter with this young mother made me realise the huge effect example can have one on another. So often we fear being bold about our Faith, but the effect of example can often have a much more profound effect than any proselytising or bible-bashing.

In more recent years, I had an influx of grandchildren staying while their parents attended to a family problem. As I saw them to bed, there was a gentle reminder about their night prayers. The response was dismaying, and from one in particular:

"I don't do prayers".
"I thought you went to a Christian school? Don't you say prayers at assembly or mealtimes?"
"Yes, but I don't do prayers at home."
"Why not?"
"Because Mummy doesn't, and I do what Mummy does".

I felt I could not take this any further other than to say they should at least thank Jesus for Mummy and Daddy and all the good things that had happened in the day. If I pushed the matter any further they would think I was a bit of an old "fuddy-duddy, or "off my head", as seem to be the common terms used by children when they can't see any logic to what their elders are saying.

Feeling something of a failure in my ability to evangelise, I mentioned this at the next Prayer meeting. Someone very wisely said: "You sow the seeds, God does the rest". It made me feel a whole lot better. Example and trust, two virtues so easily overlooked.

Anti Religion

Two of my grandchildren are not even baptised, the others have been christened in the Anglian Church. My children seemingly do not have much time for religion – being anti-Catholic in particular. Something happened in their earlier days when still at home which profoundly affected us all as a family, me in particular - so much so that I was struck dumb, literally, for 48 hours, by the maliciously contrived accusations laid on me. When the devastating accusations were discovered to be totally unfounded, there was no explanation, and no apology. Ranks closed. It completely shattered my trust in the hierarchy and my less understanding children turned away from the Catholic Church completely.

Fortunately, I had a strong enough relationship with God because of the experience that had occurred in my 'teens. I could, therefore, manage without dependence on the Church – the religion side of things – although I didn't abandon it altogether. I had looked around at various other Churches, but finally decided that better the one I knew than the ones that I didn't – they all seemed to have certain faults and failings.

For many years after, if asked, I would claim I was a Christian first and foremost and a Catholic by default. Mass and the Eucharist kept me hanging in. I think this is why I warmed so whole-heartedly to

162

the Charismatic arm of the Church; so authentic, genuine and supportive.

I had received no closure on the event that had shaken me to the core, and left me totally disillusioned with the Church - and it was not for want of trying to obtain it in the earlier days. After banging my head against a brick wall for many months, the only option left was to bury the incident deep down and try and forget about it. It was twenty-three years later before I began to realise the damaging effect this disaffection with the Church was having on my overall spirituality. I hadn't realised how far I had drifted into my own thinking.

A new direction I was taking brought the 23-year-old incident bubbling back to the surface. I was drawn to becoming a secular Franciscan and, as such, I was supposed to embrace Mother Church, warts and all, as St Francis had done. I knew I could not do this without the incident of the past being resolved. I felt I needed restorative justice so that I could understand and, therefore, hopefully forgive the priest that had caused me so much damage all those years before - but I was unsure how to go about achieving it.

Once again, I tried to seek help but felt it could not be gained from within the Diocese, as I did not wish to cause untoward scandal. My Formation Minister suggested a Franciscan retreat centre in Derbyshire run by a very wise Franciscan nun, Sr. Patricia, who, he thought, might be able to help.

Miraculous Healing

A few days before leaving for Derbyshire, I attended a Charismatic event. During Exposition we were told we could, as we felt moved, come up and kneel before the Blessed Sacrament which had been surrounded by a humeral veil. We were encouraged to make whatever prayer we wished whilst kissing the veil. My rebellious self thought: "This isn't for me – I can pray just as well where I am".

Besides, there was the practical problem I would have bending down to kneel or, more particularly, getting back up again.

During Exposition, the Prayer Teams were available for individual prayer. When this finished, my prayer partner said he hadn't been up to the Blessed Sacrament and I found myself saying that neither had I. I followed him up to the altar and, contrary to my earlier thoughts, I bent to kiss the veil and made a fervent prayer that my time in Derbyshire would give me answers to my problem of how to achieve justice and explanations and thereby lead me to forgiveness. I returned to my place at the back where I remained standing as some gentle praise singing took place.

Before a few minutes had elapsed, the perpetrator of the events all those years ago, whose presence I had been previously unaware of, was standing by my side and had placed his arm around me. Being of a very traditional nature he was certainly not one normally to attend charismatic events. I received a big hug as he mumbled something in my ear. I was so surprised and overcome, I didn't even catch what he said. On reflection, I sensed this was the only way he felt capable of offering an apology for his part in the events of twenty-three years earlier. I had never experienced such an immediate response to prayer, and could not stop myself shedding tears of joy at the release.

It was a great start to my healing, but I still felt I needed explanations. Sr. Patricia had advised against confronting this person directly, despite his initial approach. However, the explanations were to come from a different source. A short time after my visit to Derbyshire, the right person to assist me was placed in an appropriate position for approachability. I had no idea at the time just how right a person he was – he turned out to be closely involved with the perpetrator as there were ongoing health issues. This time, explanations were given for the behaviour that had caused such deep wounds, and eventually

I could forgive completely these gross historic hurts. The Church, thankfully, is changing for the better and becoming more humble and inclusive.

I can forgive my children their position on religion, bearing in mind the length of time it took me to get over the incident. I had the advantage of a strong belief in God. Regardless of their stance, they lead the equivalent of very good Christian lives. My son and his wife, who profess to be atheists, have a more Christian ethic than many – being scrupulously moral, caring for the future of the planet, caring about what they eat, always recycling and reusing resources, etc. I often tease them that they operate more purely in the Franciscan tradition than many a Franciscan.

~

REFLECTION:

FORGIVENESS & HEALING

Jesus spent His mission advocating forgiveness, being ever mindful of the frailty of human-kind. (Matt 6:14-15; Mark 11:25). He forgave sins that would have been considered heinous by society in His time. To the woman accused of adultery and about to be stoned to death, as was the punishment of the time, He exclaimed "Let he who is without sin cast the first stone". When her accusers all turned away, He told her "Go, and sin no more" (Matt 9:5).

When we are badly treated or unjustly accused, forgiveness is not easy. It can be helpful to try and understand where the perpetrator is coming from. What has caused him/her to make the false accusation, to behave in that way? Does he/she believe the behaviour to be justified, and, if so, for what reasons? Maybe they are acting on untruths fed to them by others? Have they misinterpreted a situation? What is their personal situation that may have led them to such action?

Trying to fathom some reasons for the hurt that has been caused can begin the healing. The forgiveness is often harder. Yet Jesus urges that we should forgive "not seven times but seventy-seven times" (Matt 18:21-22).

During His three years of ministry, Jesus endured criticism, unjustified accusations, and threats to His life. Sometimes He used strong words against His accusers. But in His darkest hour, as He hung crucified and in horrendous pain, He Himself forgave His transgressors: "Father forgive them for they know not what they do." (Luke 23:34).

THOUGHTS FOR DISCUSSION

1. How easy is it to forgive when no apology is forthcoming from those who caused the injury?

2. How aware are we that our behaviour can have strong repercussions, good or bad, on those around us, even though it may not be apparent at the time?

3. Do you know any person who believes they are unforgivable? Could you persuade them otherwise?

--ooOoo--

Chapter 9

CONFUSION

INTERESTING INCIDENTS

The Chair on Wheels

I hated being identified by my chair – in fact, I hated my chair except for the comfort it afforded. It came with the added aid to my comfort of a pressure relief cushion and a similar back cushion with lumbar support. The chair became as much an essential part of me as was my spine. I was either there with the chair or I was absent because, for whatever reason, the chair could not be accommodated.

People always knew when I was driving around because of the giant mosquito-like object stuck, limpet-like, to the rear of the car. When arriving at a venue, I would walk in pushing the chair as much as a prop for walking, as for its need for the duration of the sitting event. People very kindly offered me a place to park it and were naturally confused when I explained I needed it to sit in.

At parties and other social events, people would default behind the chair so I was unable to be part of their conversation. The handles behind, designed for pushing, also made convenient leaning posts, and if one person was leaning on a handle, then the others would, by default, gravitate around them. They were seemingly unaware that I would like, just as much as they, to be part of the discussion in hand. Because of my condition and its restrictions, I could not turn in the chair to join in. If I managed to draw their attention (because I could not turn my head or the chair), I would ask them to come forward of the chair, and they would do so, but it did not take long before they gradually drifted back to the 'leaning posts' behind.

I suppose it is understandable that people find it hard to accept that one could walk but still needed a wheelchair, and only for sitting. And not an ordinary wheelchair, but one with a reclining high back and head support. Standing was almost impossible, but walking somehow opened the vertebrae and was thus more comfortable than having them stacked one upon another, with no, or very little, protection in between which is what causes the discomfort. The muscles work three or four times harder than they should, because they are compensating for the weak skeleton, and it seems to be the overworked muscles which can cause much of the pain and discomfort.

Insensitivity

Those who were particularly obtuse about accepting my condition, and particularly the wheelchair, were members of my own family. They looked on the latter as some sort of monstrosity – which, to some extent it was, and they were not very prepared to accommodate it.

One of my siblings was holding a birthday party. He had made special arrangements for the wheelchair to be brought in through a garden door and on to a dust sheet – in a room not exactly at the hub of the party, but it was preferable for him so that it did not have to go through the house, fuelling his fear it might soil or damage his carpet. For years after, he remembered and complained about the dents left by the wheels that he said had remained in his carpet thereafter where the wheelchair had been located.

On another occasion, my sister had asked me to join her and her husband for a night at a smart hotel on the North Norfolk coast. I arrived before they did. I had established that there was no problem with me using the chair in the dining room, and one of the staff was extracting it from the car just as my sister and brother-in-law arrived. The latter got out of his car, and his first words to me were: "You're not using that monstrosity here!" "Why ever not?" I replied. He mumbled something about it being an up-market hotel. I reminded him that this was Norfolk, and, despite what might happen in his circles, people here were very civilised – and, anyway, what about the boot on his leg? He had strained some ligaments and had a heavy surgical boot on his right foot. "I've got an injury" he replied. "What do you think I have?" I retorted. My invisible condition was very hard to comprehend – if I was embarrassed by it, I suppose it was understandable that others were too.

I also remember discovering, some years after the event, and after she had died, that I had not been invited to a close friend's 60th birthday party. The reasons for this were not clear. She had the beginnings of a brain tumour at the time. Had this caused her to overlook a few people? Or was it my chair that would overcrowd her event? If the latter, then at least it would have been a courtesy to invite me and say: "…but there won't be room for your wheelchair." This would have been less hurtful than being left off the list of invitees altogether. I would at least have had the option, either to decline the invitation if I didn't think I would be able to cope, or to offer to join her celebration for a little while at least until I could no longer manage. I prefer to think her brain tumour was the reason for the omission.

Too Many Brains

The neck brace, if anything, caused worse embarrassment than the chair. Again, it wasn't the norm, unlike the soft collars that people with arthritic necks wear. It was made from a solid, plastic-like material, and it held the neck and head in a rigid position. It gave enormous relief to my neck. It was the same style as those used for victims of traffic accidents or serious falls. The soft collars gave me insufficient support, but there came a time when I had to wear the brace for shorter and shorter periods as the rear part aggravated the upper spine as the condition travelled its way into the upper thoracic area. Even breathing at this stage became painful as the discs in the thoracic area became affected. I understood this was quite rare as the ribs normally helped in supporting the vertebrae in their natural positions, regardless of disc condition.

Children, in particular, would comment on the neck brace and often they would ask their parents why I was wearing that 'odd thing' around my head. Once I became more confident wearing the brace in public, I had a ready reply for them. Jokingly I would tell them I had to wear it because I had too many brains which resulted in my head being too heavy for my neck to support it. This latter, to some extent, was true, though I don't believe the brains were quite as plentiful as I was implying. The perplexed children looked even more bemused!

Halleluiah!

An amusing occurrence happened, the tale of which my Mother never tired of its retelling. My friends and I decided we would like to attend the concert "Halleluiah for Hospices" which was being held at Norwich Cathedral in the year 1995. It was very crowded as we arrived, so I agreed to being pushed in my wheelchair as I was no good at slow-walking or standing in queues. We found our seats, and the one allocated for me remained spare.

Eventually, a single, middle-aged man came up and asked if the unused seat was available, to which we agreed, and he sat down. He seemed incredibly shy and, despite our attempts at being friendly, we could not raise other than a few monosyllables from him. The concert began, and at the interval he disappeared. I needed to visit the Ladies and my friends asked if they should push me in the chair. I declined their offer as I needed a bit of movement, having sat for so long, so off I went with just my sticks.

On my return, there was a bit of a commotion. The user of the spare seat had returned and was shocked to find the empty wheelchair beside him. Apparently, he thought he had witnessed a miracle! I duly sat down and tried to explain my condition to him. He was so animated as a result of his experience, even though it was not the miracle he had thought, that it was hard to stop him talking from then on, even when the concert restarted.

Unusual high-backed, reclining back, maroon-coloured wheelchair, with leg raisers, and a neck brace – no surprise his reaction, I suppose. He had just failed to notice the sticks I had with me too.

Lourdes

At my Mother's behest, I went on a pilgrimage to Lourdes – this was to be a new experience for me. Mum was obviously hoping a miracle cure truly would occur this time! As a dutiful daughter, and with some financial help from her towards the fare, I embarked on the Diocesan Pilgrimage in 1995 with my friend, Penny, as my escort.

It was not a good experience. I hated being there. Every evening we would take a walk down to the Domain after supper, and I would end up in floods of tears. I could not bear all the illness, disability and sickness that surrounded me in such a concentrated form. A terrible sadness would overcome me for all the sufferers, many or most of whom had far worse conditions than mine, and I fail to remember what I thought about God at the time.

At home I could feel relatively normal with my home being specially equipped with suitable chairs and other largely unnoticeable aids and props around me, and the freedom to move around, lie down, or sit, as and when and how my body demanded. I lived as normal a life as my differently abled body allowed, masked by pain relief. In Lourdes, I was just another of the disabled or sick.

I hated the title "Disabled" and there it was, in Lourdes, a constant rubbing of my nose in it. Fortunately, we had great fun at meal times as we had our very down-to-earth and humorous Bishop, Peter Smith, (now Archbishop) sharing our table – he sat at the head and I was placed opposite him at the foot of the table, and some great good clean jokes, as well as wine, were shared. I had my better wheelchair by this time, though still very unusual, and he was fascinated by it, wanting to know how to dismantle it so he could help load it onto the coach when the time came to return home.

Does She Take Sugar?

The afternoon we were to have the special service for the sick and disabled was an incident indelibly etched on my mind. I appreciated the blessings that would come from such a service but, again, I was being expressly labelled as one of the "Sick". To compound my discomfort, our Parish curate, who oversaw the organising of this service, came up to my friend at lunchtime and asked her: "Does Anne want to receive the Sacrament of the Sick this afternoon?" I was very taken aback as he was fully aware of my capabilities, particularly the fact that I could talk and hear!! I responded before my friend could do so. "Excuse me, Father, that smacks of 'Does she take sugar'!"

This curate had been a nurse before he took Holy Orders. He knew my capabilities well, particularly that I had a fully functioning mouth with equally operational vocal chords. He should have known better and he was duly mortified. But then the chair and neck brace were enough to make anyone think, even momentarily, that I was far more incapacitated than I was.

This service, and many others, was among some beautiful experiences in Lourdes, but again I was always obliged to be lumped in an area designated for the sick and disabled which I disliked intensely. At Mass back home, I and my wheelchair would find a suitable spot where we would not be too much of an obstruction amongst the general congregation, and most of the time I could walk the short distance to receive Holy Communion. It would not have been 'de riguer' to do this at the Domain services.

Don't Cause a Miracle!

Another more practical problem with Lourdes was my need to keep what little mobility I had functioning. Because of the large numbers attending the services, they were very long, and I found myself in a sitting position for far too long. I would normally try to walk as much as possible in between services or other occasions requiring long periods of sitting. This was something I desperately needed to do to gain a modicum of comfort and retain some general mobility.

Within the Domain I had to be very mindful that if I got out of the wheelchair after a service, as I would normally have done after a lengthy period of sitting elsewhere, people might think, like the poor man at Norwich Cathedral, that they were witnessing a miracle – particularly as this was Lourdes. Consequently, Lourdes, despite its services and prayerful occasions, was not the ideal place for someone with my condition as I found myself having to sit for periods well in excess of what was good for me, and that increased my discomfort.

ALTERNATIVE HEALTHCARE

Susan

Of far more benefit to me than the trip to Lourdes was the remedial, or deep tissue massage my Mother paid for until she departed this world and left me an inheritance which, after 25 years, pays for it still.

After my final, and devastating diagnosis, and the subsequent visit to my Mother's surgeon, the Professor in Orthopaedics, an Aunt, who had been a nurse in her younger years, advised that I should have some remedial massage. The National Health Service had all but wiped their hands off me except for palliative care and the niggardly availability of further access to Consultants if the condition threw up new problems.

At the recommendation of a friend, I came to meet this wonderful, highly qualified lady named Susan. Her treatments were not cheap but it was not very long before I came to learn that she was worth every penny. At the time, I could not afford to pay for her treatment myself, my business having only just recently come into profit, which is why my Mother offered.

My Mother could not understand why I could not have this costly deep tissue massage - which I have fortnightly, and even more frequently when the need arises, paid for by the National Health Service. I could see that the cost/benefit return in terms of their resources made it not feasible as there were other patients with more life-threatening conditions in greater need, and patients where positive results could be more assured and more speedily obtained.

Learning to Cope

My visits to Susan were weekly for the first few years, and initially – probably because I was still depressed - I remember quietly sobbing as she worked her way across my wrecked body. She was very empathetic and taught me how to 'live within my capabilities' rather than keep on trying to do the impossible. In my mind, it was not the impossible - I was merely trying to live as one would expect from someone my age, but my body was not commensurate with my age.

I had to start living differently, and consider my body's needs more, and rest more. Is it tired of standing? Then sit. When uncomfortable sitting, then move about. If necessary, lie down. I was not used to a lazy lifestyle, nor one dictated to by my body rather than my diary, particularly having been so sporty and energetic in my youth.

Lunch hours during work were extended so that I could take longer rest periods and I had to learn to delegate some of the property visits to the staff. I still made sure I met every new landlord myself. A stick became a useful aid, particularly when standing, as I then had something to lean on. The stick became a prop for my spine.

Not coping

I came to observe that if I was trying to sit on anything other than in my wheelchair where I could recline, my posture resembled that of a 90-year-old, leaning forward with two hands on my stick for support. Reclining and leaning forward were means of taking the pressure off my vertebrae. Arthritis was also beginning to attack other parts of my body. My wrists and thumbs were becoming increasingly painful, as were hips, shoulders and feet (the latter being somewhat mal-formed anyway). I got to the point where I was seriously beginning to think I needed a live-in carer, or the alternative of having to book into a care home. I wasn't managing on my own, despite some basic assistance given by my staff and whoever happened to be lodging at the time. I wasn't even 50 years old.

Many have criticised the lack of support from my family when I needed it most, but they all lived at a distance (125 miles being the nearest) and they had young families with their own cares and concerns to cope with. Even my brothers and sisters, all being younger than me, had young families - one brother has a child born six months after my first grandchild. A counsellor once told me she found my independence surprising as I was from such a large family: "You have become too independent - people don't see your need."

Casualty

A rather amusing incident occurred one evening on my return from a very Spirit-filled prayer evening - although initially it was a bit scary. It was a very wet, miserable night. As I was approaching the outer side of a bend, a car suddenly appeared, coming towards me at great speed on the wrong side of the road as it overtook two other cars on the bend. I pulled over to the verge as best I could to avoid a collision, but nonetheless the car glanced me quite a heavy blow which caused it to waver, and then it drove off.

The drivers of the two cars that had been overtaken had witnessed what happened, and both came over to see if they could help. One of the guys happened to be an off-duty paramedic. He spotted my neck brace and insisted that I mustn't move despite my worries regarding the fluid leaking from the front of my car. I thought this could have been petrol but he assured me it was water from the radiator. He insisted on calling an ambulance despite my protestations that I was fine.

I could but do as I was told. Everything was happening around me as I continued sitting in my driver's seat, feeling a bit like an actor in a scene from the TV series 'Casualty'. Eventually I had to allow myself to be stretchered into an ambulance whereupon a policeman came in to question me about the incident – or so I thought. His words were: "I know this is going to add insult to injury but I have to breathalyse you." In my slightly euphoric state, and without thinking, I replied: "The only spirit you'll find on me is the Holy Spirit!". He must have thought the accident truly had affected me!

At the hospital, I was not allowed to move, even to go to the toilet, until I was seen by a doctor. They had no pillows available, so the experience was far from comfortable, lying on my back on a hard couch with my bad neck still in its brace. I was also told on no account should I take the brace off so without a pillow it caused quite a strain to the upper thoracic area. Eventually a doctor gave me a cursory check-over and I was told I could go home. It was past midnight and I had no car – after all the fuss I was suddenly left high and dry to find myself a taxi!

BUSINESS MATTERS

Coping

It seemed ironic that, as my business grew, giving me the wherewithal to start enjoying the things in life that I had been deprived of for so many years because of financial constraints, my disability grew worse. In terms of how I was coping, it was at times hard but I was determined not to give up. I could still just about walk – sufficiently to get around the properties so long as I didn't have to stand still. Invariably I perched on windowsills when chatting to clients (most properties under my care were unfurnished).

I used to think that someone in my state should never have been responsible for so many properties that were mostly my clients' largest life-time investments. But then I had good staff that I could rely on. We were a team – I could not have carried on without their faithful support. I did, however, have one or two non-starters over the years, who did not last very long in my employ.

Bad Vibes

If I attended business meetings I did feel rather silly in the wheelchair provided by the National Health Service – the red, reclining, high-backed one, with adjustable arms and leg raisers - especially when I did not have a companion or escort with me. Technically I could

177

walk, and dismount the wheelchair from its tow bar contraption myself. Remounting it involved more muscular effort which, again, I could do, but should ideally refrain from doing as it caused a certain amount of muscular effort, and one never knew what longer term effect that could lead to.

I suppose that if I was bull-headed enough to keep my business going despite my condition, I should be bull-headed enough to feel at ease despite my bizarre appearance – ie resembling a crash victim in a less-than-ordinary wheelchair, with neck brace and special cushions for support - the lot. But I could walk, and needed to get up and move about from time to time to prevent the muscles and spine lapsing into a particularly uncomfortable state, and even seizing up altogether.

People didn't quite know how to respond and I would remain in isolation feeling an idiot. Eventually the day came when I thought: "I don't care anymore what people think" and went to a business meeting with a pillow for support for my neck (as well as the brace). Amazingly, the other attendees came up offering to fetch me cups of tea, talked to me, offered to help, etc. I could only assume that my previous state of being ill-at-ease with myself must have made it uncomfortable for people to approach me. As my barriers were now down, so too, it seemed, were the barriers to approachability.

Customer Confidence

At the few business meetings I attended, the purpose, if not for extended learning, was for networking. In a promotional environment, the nature of the wheelchair - which doubled as my office chair - did little to encourage an outsider's confidence in my ability to look after their properties. For the office, I eventually sought a specialist chair to replace the use of the wheelchair - a proper piece of furniture that would offer me the support I needed without casting doubt on my capability as manager of a sole proprietor business.

The chair that seemed the most suitable was going to cost a sum greater than £800. One of my friends had a son who had trained at the London School of Osteopathy. She suggested I visit the School to check out my options before paying out so much money. They apparently had an advisory department where they also sold a variety of furniture and aids for people with musculoskeletal problems.

The Tourist Trail.

My son and I set off for London one hot sunny day during the summer holidays. We packed a lunch and some soft drinks to have in the car. My condition, was by then, at a point where travel by train and the consequent walking would have been impossible, whereas my car seat, with headrest and cushion to fill the gap, gave the support I required.

It was quite fun as we followed the open-topped tour bus through Central London and along the Embankment, with the sun beating down through the open sunroof of the car. We were travelling at a pace that allowed us to eat our picnic lunch in relative comfort and ease, and to take in the famous London landmarks, at no cost to us except for the petrol. Eventually, we reached our destination near St Paul's Cathedral and I was able to park right outside the School of Osteopathy with my Disability Badge.

The London School of Osteopathy

We were in the School of Osteopathy for well-nigh three hours as a specialist asked details about my condition, and gave me so much useful information, whilst my son paced around the showroom area somewhat bored. I was shown various aids and chairs to try, all of which were excessively expensive. The chair most suited to my needs, the assistant claimed, would cost me the best part of £1,000.

Towards the end of the afternoon, as I obviously appeared somewhat hesitant about ordering the chair in view of the cost, the assistant asked if I was in the PACT scheme. This was something I knew nothing about, so he proceeded to explain that I could get Government assistance with any business-related needs required to keep me able to work. He was sure I would qualify and that the PACT organisation would provide a suitable chair for me. This was great news, but I was a little sceptical as my condition was one that did not seem to have a specific label to it, and did not quite fit into the usual 'disabled' categories.

Parking Problems

Over the years, I had had considerable difficulties qualifying for the Green Badge for parking (nowadays the new European standard badges are blue) as the ridged rules precluded me because I had a modicum of walking ability, despite my prescribed need for a wheelchair.

The Assistant at the School, obviously interested in my condition, asked how we had travelled from Norfolk and I explained we had the car outside to which he seemed somewhat surprised. Apparently, the Green Badges for disability parking were not applicable in London – one had to have a London residents' disability parking permit.

On exiting the building, I was delighted to note that no parking ticket had been appended to the windscreen and we began our journey home – in the belief that the day had been a great success, and I was very grateful to my son for his company (I may even have bribed him for the privilege!).

Even had we been blighted with a parking ticket, it would have been a small price to pay for the huge amount of money I was eventually to save, and the increase in comfort afforded, thanks to the information I had been given about PACT. It was so refreshing to know that despite the length of time the School's representative had spent with me, he was prepared to forfeit a sale by providing me with this valuable information – maybe PACT purchased the equipment from them - who knows?

PACT

The Swedish Chair

I contacted the disability service at the Department of Employment that operated the PACT scheme. A representative came out and took all my details and assessed my needs. The chair I was offered, which suited my needs best, was a stylish piece of Swedish furniture. It was, to a large extent, a rocking chair, but the rockers had three slightly flattened areas with padded kneelers on the front ends so that one could kneel forward to work at the desk with the support for back and neck remaining in place. The mid position was for normal sitting and, if one tipped back on to the rear flat part of the rockers, the chair gave a semi-reclining position which took the weight off the base of the spine, thereby offering even more relief.

The chair was perfectly contoured to support the spine in whichever position it was in, and atop the rosewood frame, for head and neck support, there was a padded contoured roll on a slider for height adjustment. It was a beautifully elegant piece of furniture that belied its purpose. Not only did it offer support and comfort for my condition, and prestige for my office, but it also afforded a certain amount of exercise. To be able to move between the three positions, and to balance in the sitting position, one had to use a little muscular effort, aided by pushing with the feet, and so it provided a modicum of additional exercise to keep my spine mobile - even when needing to sit. Another bonus.

The Laptop

To my surprise, I was also offered a laptop. I had discovered I had a reluctance to use the computer and, for a long while, I remained puzzled as to the reason why, because I had a fascination for what they were capable of. The reason, it transpired, was because the position needed for viewing the monitor caused stress to my damaged neck.

The PACT representative had assessed that, with a laptop, I could look down onto the screen, thus opening the cervical vertebrae and thereby preventing any unnecessary additional discomfort. I could also adopt a more comfortable sitting position using a laptop, as opposed to viewing the monitor of a computer.

Because of problems with lifting, which also caused upset to the neck and upper thoracic area, I was given an expensive light-weight model. It was quite advanced for the time in that it held a whole 1Gb of memory! Even my son, whose studies at University caused him to be at the pinnacle of computing technology, did not have use of one quite that advanced.

PACT also produced a speech recognition programme to be used with the laptop so that I would not even have to type but, even with training, I found this 'Dragon Naturally Speaking' program difficult to use. I did not feel it was completely necessary for the state of my condition at that point. Even the slight arm movement involved in typing was beneficial to my condition.

Assistance

Reimbursement of expenses for any assistance I needed with the wheelchair when used for going out and about on business was also offered. Visiting properties was not too onerous a task without the wheelchair as I could walk short distances from car to property, and then perch on windowsills once inside, for short periods at least. However, I began to think of attending talks and seminars again, and events hosted by the Federation of Small Businesses that provided learning, support and networking, particularly useful for the sole owner businesses such as myself. Such events were essential to keeping abreast of the business and lettings world, and any new legislation affecting one's occupation. All these events I had more or less given up as the spine, and my embarrassment surrounding it, grew worse.

The (Blue) Chair on Wheels

To attend such meetings with the NHS wheelchair currently in my possession was never a great inspirer of confidence in what my sole-trader business could offer, particularly regarding the networking-type of gatherings. I explained this problem at one of my contact assessments with PACT and immediately was offered the chance to choose a more ergonomically acceptable wheelchair.

It was not easy to find one that would fit into the car without having adaptations made to the car. Eventually we found one that had a solid base (although the wheels could be taken off if required). The back and leg supports all lifted off for ease of storage and transportation. The head support was also removable. The maintenance person we used for the properties constructed some foldable ramps and, with minimal assistance, I could manage to get the new chair into, and out of, my estate-type car on my own.

The chair (on-wheels) was quite smart, and well-upholstered in a blue covering. It had reclining positions, an adjustable head rest, leg and arm rests, and it was very comfortable, so much so that, of an evening, it came into the house and acted as my armchair for the remainder of the day. The wheelchair was the only thing I had suggested to PACT would be beneficial. All the other aids - laptop, office chair, etc. - were volunteered by the Scheme assessors.

The Motorised Chair

Somewhere along the line I had to succumb to the use of a motorised wheelchair. I believe I was given the option of a Motability car purchase, or the motorised chair. I chose the latter. An allowance was awarded and I had to put the balance monies towards it so I opted for a second-hand one. The effort of pushing the blue upholstered chair into the back of the car was becoming increasingly difficult on my own. Walking had become ever more painful and dangerous because of the risk of falling – I had bad feet which didn't help and had begun to experience arthritis in the hips, thumbs and wrists. The motorised chair could be motored up the ramp into the back of the car. Just like the previous two chairs, it had a detachable head rest, leg raisers and, in addition, an aid for getting up kerbs smoothly. I used to refer to this as my kerb crawler.

Societal Benefits

All this help from PACT seemed very generous, but at the end of the day, for an investment on the part of the Government of some £5,000 in total over the years I needed the help, it was a relatively small outlay for the Government to keep me able to work. The benefit to the Government was that, by keeping me in a position where I could remain in business, I could support myself, thus avoiding the need for unemployment benefit. I was also offering a useful service to the community, paying taxes, employing staff, and employing the services of other businesses - and it kept me from depression and the consequent relevant medication. It gave me an opportunity to build up something of a pension of my own, rather than become dependent on the State for that, too. It gave me a sense of purpose, a status, a sense of feeling useful to the community rather than being a burden to it.

~

REFLECTION:

BEING DIFFERENT

We are community people, social beings – we don't like being different. Sometimes we over-compensate to conform, we modify our personality to become accepted, then we are no longer our true selves - the self in the way God made us. Alternatively, we may have a physical feature or some deformity, a defect of birth, or resulting from an accident or illness, that can't be altered. Maybe even an interest or hobby that is not the 'norm' - all things that can make us stand out from the crowd, that people often find difficult to accept. Then frequently we become shunned.

God made us in His own image and likeness (Gen. 1:26). For some of us that might seem rather odd when virtually no two people look alike. I prefer to think that what is referred to is not our outward physical being but our innermost soul. We have the capacity to be God-like in our personality, though it is a hard path to follow.

We do not have the right to treat any human being differently to another just because we dislike something about their physical appearance, habits or background. God made each one of us the way we are for a purpose: "Does not the potter have the right to make out of the same lump of clay some pottery for special purposes and some for common use?" (Romans 9:21).

Everyone, therefore, should be treated alike, regardless of outward appearance or status. In each person we encounter God, whether they recognise God in themselves or not. "...whatever you did for one of the least of these brothers and sisters of Mine, you did for Me." (Matt 25:35-40)

THOUGHTS FOR DISCUSSION

1. How often do you place yourself in other's shoes to be better able to understand how they might be feeling?

2. How often does our pride, or our social standing, prevent us from engaging with our neighbour?

3. Do you think you could ever come to love everybody unreservedly, as God does?

--ooOoo--

Chapter 10

EXPANSION

GROWTH

Booming Business

By 1993 I had achieved three years' accounts showing profits – not large ones but enough to show an upward trend. For the first three years in business, I had creamed the market for managing upmarket properties, operating pretty much throughout the whole of Norfolk, and with virtually no competition. I was the only letting agent of quality, both for service and for the type of properties under my care. What I was offering was unique - and word got around. The oil boom was burgeoning off Great Yarmouth, producing a large influx of industry-related personnel who required the quality of property I was offering. Shell UK, Schlumberger, and even Norwich Union that had its own lettings facility, were among some of the personnel departments using my service. This was a bonus I could not have anticipated.

Alongside the benefits of the 1988 Housing Act, the state of the economy at the time, although sadly detrimental to most, was a bonus to my type of business too, because it created a new variety of tenant. Some were homeowners who were finding themselves in financial difficulties and had defaulted on their mortgages. They were being repossessed at phenomenal rates. These unfortunate people still needed a roof over their, and their family's heads. Once the mortgage company had claimed their dues, quite often these families had some capital remaining from the sale of their once-treasured investment, thereby making them financially viable as tenants. Being previous homeowners also, they knew how to, and were more likely to, respect and care for property belonging to others.

There were also new types of landlord: those making their properties available for let because they were being transferred abroad by their companies and wished to return to their homes after their secondment, and those who had found themselves to be in negative equity and unable to sell, despite having to move to a new area. We were also experiencing the first generation of property inheritors. These people often had sentimental attachments to the inherited property that had once belonged to a parent or other relative and they were not ready to entertain the thought of selling them.

All these rental properties provided the accommodation for those who had lost their homes through repossession, or for those having to move into a new area and were unable to sell in their previous locality. Although it was a gradual progression, the 1988 Housing Act had provided homeowners with confidence to become landlords. Even the owners of property purchased merely as investment prior to 1988, were re-launching their portfolios onto the market for rent after years of reluctance resulting from their inability to evict tenants when the necessity arose because of the way legal system had operated. Times were changing in a big way and I, by mere chance, had been there at the fore. Mere chance...?

Business Image

Despite having to work from home I attempted to portray as business-like an image as possible – even more important bearing in mind the not-so-business-like premises and person running it.

Provided I could get out of bed, which I attempted each morning, albeit with a struggle, I was in the office for 9am, and there I mostly remained there until 5.30pm. A lunch break was religiously taken, mainly for rest purposes, and there were trips out to visit properties for the various purposes connected with the agency work. I could not do much in terms of networking or other forms of physically promoting the business, but the properties came in regardless. Some clients contacted me only by phone or mail and would, therefore, be totally unaware of my condition, or the fact that mine was a small business technically operating from home – unless, of course, they had done some thorough research. But there were others…..

Cottage Industry?

Despite my good reputation, there were some around who seemed to consider I might be nothing more than a 'here today, gone tomorrow' cottage-type industry, and I know I lost some business as a consequence. The husband of a friend of mine, who was MD of the local branch of a large national company, visited me one day to discuss some property he had available for let. The interview took place in what was my tiny dining room converted into a working office. One comment he made which I particularly recall was: "I don't see you in 'Yellow Pages'. I think he saw this as some measure of permanency as a company. Very shortly afterwards, I laid out some not inconsiderable sum for advertisements in two categories in this directory, 'Properties to let' and 'Accommodation', and these we recommissioned annually. Previously, I had no need for such advertising but competition was beginning to bite.

I did not get this gentleman's business. I don't believe it was my lack of a presence in 'Yellow Pages' alone that caused his lack of confidence – the 'premises' and its access could not have enhanced his trust in the capabilities or permanence of Heron. When I originally bought the bungalow, it had to be done rather hastily and was not my ideal choice for a home. It was small, and not suited to us as a family, let alone for incorporating a business, the germination of which had not even begun at the time of its purchase. The property was meant to have been a stopgap - it had never been my intention to stay there longer than necessary, and I had always felt I was doing little more than camping in it. It never felt like 'home'.

Now I needed to improve my business image and the access for customers - I needed something better and more conveniently located. I needed somewhere where premises for the business would be attached to, but separate from, the house; something with an attached double garage or outbuildings that could be suitably converted into offices. Looking around, it seemed that only something of the nature of a four-bedroomed property would have such a facility but, even with my three years' accounts, I could not substantiate the mortgage required to support the meagre deposit I could raise from the sale of the bungalow.

MOVING THE BUSINESS

Insurance Benefits

One of the facilities I offered my landlords – indeed, actively encouraged them towards - was a special insurance to cover them in the event of problems with a tenant. This was known as a legal protection insurance and covered them for solicitors' and court fees in the event of problems such as unpaid-for damage, non-payment of rent, and, if the need arose - for eviction. This was of great benefit to me because, as soon as a problem manifested itself, and our dealings direct with the tenant failed to resolve the problem, we could immediately hand over to the insurance company who had their own experienced legal team that took over all the necessary procedures.

Only twice during the whole time I ran the business – some 18 years – did I have to attend Court as the landlord's representative whilst his insurer's solicitors handled the proceedings. The second time I attended, I remember asking the solicitor what seemed to him a basic question. He was most surprised when I told him I had only attended such proceedings once before. Most agents, he told me, attended Court on a regular basis for eviction or non-payment.

Catch 22

A very annoying element of the law was that a tenant had to be at least two months in arrears with their rent before they could be taken to Court. What inevitably happens is that a wily tenant would pay a small sum the day before, or even on the morning of the Court proceedings - enough to bring the overdue amount to just below the two months-worth of arrears, and the case would have to be abandoned. These cases would cause untold expenditure, both of time and money, to a landlord's legal insurance company - assuming the landlord had been wise enough to avail himself of this facility, and if not, then to the landlord himself. And the ploy could be utilised repeatedly by the same unscrupulous tenants.

Insurance Pays – In Many Ways

The insurance company I dealt with had a representative, a lovely girl, who was a refugee from Rhodesia. Prior to one of her visits, she announced that she was leaving the company to pursue other interests, and asked if she could bring along for introduction a colleague who was to become her successor.

The new rep and I got along famously. At the end of our chat he said to me; "If there is anything else I can help you with, please let me know." I was unsure if he was referring to my disability, or merely my business. In the next breath, he told me he had previously been a mortgage expert among other things. Very tongue in cheek, I told him of my dream of moving premises and the amount I was likely to require as a mortgage.

To my great surprise, he took me seriously and said he might be able to help as he still had contacts in the business. I told him I realised my disability might be held against me, but I assured him I had managed the business from my bed before. I also assured him I would only need the larger property for the time I was running the business, after which I could downsize and repay the mortgage with the proceedings. I also mentioned that, somewhere in the future, there was likely to be a bit of an inheritance at the demise of my Mother. "Leave it with me," says he. And they both left - he with copies of my three years' accounts. I was convinced that, once he studied my accounts, he would come to the reality of the situation, so I did not think any further about it.

A few days later, I received a phone call from the said representative. "I have received an offer in principle for you," he announced. "However, to fit the repayments to your current income, the repayments would span 40 years. How do you feel about that?" I realised that, without any intervening lump sum repayments, I would be 90 before the mortgage became fully repaid. "Is this for real?" or words to that effect, was my response. He told me that had I gone to any high-street building society or bank they would not even looked at the proposal. With his reputation in, and knowledge of, the industry he was able to persuade a small East Anglian building society that I was a safe bet to invest in, bearing in mind, I am sure, the information I had given him about my abilities (which he had to some extent witnessed for himself), and my future intentions, and prospects of inheritance.

House Hunting

I was over the moon. Now befell to me the task of trying to find somewhere suitable to purchase. I decided it needed to be close to where we currently lived to maintain the link with the area, both from a personal and business point of view. It needed an adjoining building, either garage or attached outhouses, because, at that time, it negated the need to pay business rates. I now knew what my mortgage capability was (!!), and I knew roughly what I could achieve from the sale of the bungalow (less current mortgage) to act as a deposit.

It was not easy. Properties for sale in Brundall sold like hot-cakes because of its popularity. Mostly, they did not even reach the market as purchasers were waiting on the side lines, and the local well-fed grapevine would alert them that someone was planning to sell. I discovered, too, that properties in Brundall were more expensive than in the surrounding villages because of the benefits of the railway, bus service, riverside, good school and abundant community facilities – which, of course, is what made it such a popular place to live. Residents who were obliged to move away for business reasons, or even from choice, would often discover a desire to return to Brundall, and frequently did so when the opportunity arose, particularly for retirement.

I needed somewhere on a fairly busy, easily accessible road. I found myself mainly viewing properties in Blofield, the neighbouring, conjoined village where like-for-like properties were an average 20% cheaper. What had been the A47 main trunk road between Birmingham and Great Yarmouth had passed through the middle of the village, cutting it in half, until bypassed in the early 'nineties, whereupon the old road was briefly re-labelled the Old Yarmouth Road. Now it has become simply the main road through the village, linked at either end to the Bypass. A property on, or just off, this road seemed to be a good option.

The property I was looking for, I decided, needed to be roughly within a three-mile radius to achieve continuity for the business. It also needed to be suitable for my own personal requirements. I liked properties with a certain amount of character and I was a great fan of south-facing gardens. However, needs must - I could not afford to be too picky. I vowed I would view anything within my price bracket with the required appendage suitable for the business.

Ideal Home

There was one property I nearly overlooked as it was modern, on a small estate, plain, and rectangular in shape, and altogether rather characterless. However, the search, so far, had proved somewhat fruitless. I decided I should look at it regardless.

As soon as I walked into the hall I realised the character was inside, not out. It had double glass doors to the lounge (ideal for wheelchair access) at a slight angle to the hall which added character. It had an open-flame gas fire that, when lit, was impossible to tell it was not a real fire – so much easier for me to manage than clearing ashes from a coal fire that would have been my preference in different circumstances.

Some eight years earlier, the property had been the show house on this modest development. As such, it had the largest garden because it incorporated the piece of land that would have been an isolated triangle. The estate was surrounded by three roads forming the triangle, and the neighbouring rectangular plots backed onto this triangular piece of garden – so there were, in total, seven neighbouring properties!

The garden, therefore, had an interesting shape and it was south-facing. Another advantage was an amazing view across the Yare Valley from the south-facing upstairs rooms. The property was well built, with quality refinements. Inside, the woodwork, skirting, doors, etc. were painted in a rich mahogany colour adding a touch of elegance. It was very well appointed, with plenty of sockets, and other fine touches. The only disappointment was the family bathroom which had a builder's suite of bath, loo and basin in differing shades

194

of white - obviously a bargain lot. Above all, it had an attached double garage….

I made an offer. The family was Australian and wished to return to their native country. I had yet to sell my own property. The vendors and I seemed to get on well and they were prepared to wait. They even gave me their telephone number so that I could keep them directly informed of progress with the sale of my own property.

The Burst Bubble

I expected my property to sell quite quickly. Eighteen months down the line, I had not received a sensible offer. The kitchen and bathroom needed updating, so I decided to get this in hand in the hope that it would help with the selling. Failing that, at least we, as a family, would benefit from the improvements.

To my surprise, the property sold soon after the new installations were effected. I then realised I would have to start my search anew as the Australian family had long since decided to withdraw their property from the market – my dream home - and stay put.

Nothing suitable seemed to materialise. Maybe I was still focussed on the property that fitted the bill in almost every way, with only the bathroom that disappointed. It also had a sloping drive but I had decided that installing steps up to pavement level was not an impossibility. I even asked the builder of the estate, who was still constructing similar properties along the road, whether he was prepared to build another to the same specification as No 38, but it seemed he could not – planning permission presumably having been already obtained for the remaining plots.

Eureka!

Then another eureka moment occurred – why not ring the Australians to see if they just might change their minds? It was a shot in the dark with, in my estimation, a less than five per cent chance of success. I still had their number. Heart in mouth, I dialled and got Mrs R... I blurted out my thoughts and awaited the inevitable rejection. After all, there must have been some good reason why they had decided not to return to Australia as originally planned. To my great surprise, she said she would have a word with her husband.

That same evening, I received the return call. Yes, they were willing to sell!! I could not believe my ears! We arranged a time for me to revisit. I was amazed to find the bathroom, my one disappointment, had been completely revamped. It now had a modern suite (matching in colour!) and even more fabulous - a wide corner bath with a seat. This would make bathing so much easier for me as there would be room for turning over on to my knees in the bath to aid getting out, and the seat would be very helpful too. It was surrounded by beautiful, modern, feature tiling – a true luxury! Some One truly had my interests at heart.

Even better, the Aussies were prepared to keep to the price we had previously agreed, despite any inflation and the improvements that had taken place in the intervening two years - and there was no need for estate agent's fees. They even offered to split the fee-difference with me. I may have had an unfortunate amount of bad luck in my life but I have had also an equal, even exceptional, amount of good fortune. The circumstances surrounding the acquisition of this property seemed almost beyond belief - God was truly on my side.

TRULY HOME?

Madness

My friends thought I was crazy. They had known of my intention to move but seemingly disbelieved I would go ahead with the plan. Why did I want to move from a bungalow to a house involving stairs, particularly with my disability? Why, when my family had all left home by this time, did I want four bedrooms? Why did I want to move from Brundall where all my friends lived?

It was not difficult to field these questions. The house move was essentially required for the future of the business, and four bedrooms, by default, seemed the inevitable size of property needed to gain the adjoining premises required, suitable for the business. The house also had a straight set of stairs so, if necessary, a chairlift could easily be installed. Besides, I had been told that climbing stairs was a very good means of exercise for the spine - and other joints as they aged. My children were at the ages when marriage would hopefully be on the horizon and then three would turn into six, followed by, even more hopefully – grandchildren.

Regarding 'leaving behind' my friends, our bungalow had been right at the western end of the village. In fact, I hadn't even been living in Brundall at all – strictly speaking, I lived in the parish of Postwick. The parish boundary passed through my neighbour's utility room, even though the actual village centre of Postwick was three miles down the road. The estate was an appendage to Brundall, built in the late '60s. Moving to Blofield made the distance from friends, if anything, somewhat nearer as most of them lived at the eastern end of the village, and Blofield, with my new home-to-be, was just up the road linking the eastern ends of the two villages.

The Gamble

Another worry for my friends was the cost. It was not that long since I had been the penniless single mother – why take the risk? Why, indeed - it was a gamble. I knew I could survive in the new house for a minimum two years on the money I had to hand even if the business did not continue doing well.

I had to give it a go to give the business a good chance to build up the portfolio because competition was increasing at quite a rate. I was becoming more severely disabled by this time. How would I cope with a move? I was running on autopilot, trusting, and somehow I knew what I was doing had to be done.

The Move

The day came for the move. It was the 4th December 1995, and it was snowing. Because of the footpath from bungalow to the road, the removal men could not get near with their van and the furniture had to be carried down to the end of the snow-covered pathway where the van was parked.

As it became more and more slippery with their heavy footsteps flattening the snow, it took the removal men much longer than anticipated to clear the bungalow. Although they managed to get the bedrooms organised, and some other furniture correctly sorted into their proper places in the new house, most of the rest of my chattels they hurriedly piled into the kitchen and lounge as they were two hours over their allotted time.

It was well past six in the evening before they finished. The kitchen was a nightmare - impossible to reach the oven, fridge, sink, or anything else, because of furnishings and boxes. Fortunately, the date coincided with an early Book Club Christmas dinner that had been arranged back in Brundall, so I did not have to worry about the cooking – I just shut the door on the shambles and went out for the evening.

Bliss

It was great that night, having been entertained among friends, and then returning to sleep upstairs once again in what seemed like a luxury hotel room compared to what I had been used to during the previous seventeen years. The R…….s had left all the curtains so all I had to do was find some bedding.

The place had been meticulously cleaned – apparently, so I was told by the vendors, because my reputation for the cleanliness of the properties under my care had gone before me. They were not involved in any way with the rental market, and it was heartening to know that my reputation stretched beyond, as well as it was a pleasure to experience.

The Reluctant Mover

I had somehow managed to overlap the sale by two days to make the proceedings easier for myself. Although the bulky office furniture had gone over, we had time to ease the rest of business across over the next couple of days, without too much disruption. It also gave us a chance to get the bungalow properly cleaned. There was not much I could do myself – another reason some of my local friends thought I was mad to move. Others, however, put themselves out to come and help sort everything into their rightful places.

There was the very nervous elderly cat to think about, too. We left her overnight in the bungalow with which she was familiar, with her food and water in the usual place. The cat flap was locked and the staff and cleaner given instructions not to let her out when they arrived in the morning. The cat, Jenni, had always been a nightmare to get into the cat basket for visits to the vet, and those who tried either gave up, or ended up severely scratched by a terrified animal that was stronger than the human ability to hold her.

The following morning, I arrived to supervise the transfer of the final bits and bobs, including Jenni - only to find she had vanished. My colleague and a cleaner were already in the bungalow - I assumed she must have slipped out unnoticed when they arrived. I trusted she would return before too long - but she didn't. Once we had completely cleared the bungalow, and the business was safely and completely installed in the dining room of the new house, I did a final check of all the rooms to make sure all were thoroughly clean and empty. I hoped our Jenni would have returned by then too.

I found Jenni in what had been the girls' bedroom where she had spent much of her time on one or other of their beds when they were still at home. Jenni was sitting on the window sill, tucked behind the curtain (a set I had planned to leave behind), and she was shaking like a leaf, totally phased by the unusual circumstances of what had been her home. I think she had been there all day and possibly during the whole of the previous night too. For the first time ever, she slipped into the cat basket with no fuss and seemingly with a huge sense of relief.

CONVERSION

Planning Permission

I did not wish to tempt fate or upset anyone by applying for planning permission to convert the garage before the house was truly mine. I realised this was a gamble – permission could be refused. If I had applied before the purchase, would I still have gone ahead with the move if it had been turned down? Even had we had to continue running the business from the dining room (where it was first installed), we would be still in a far better location from the point of view of prestige and customer access, though it would not have been ideal.

The planning permission was not easy to obtain. The Council was worried about parking. I pointed out that, because of the way I ran the business, very few people would come to the premises. Fortunately, there was a female on the Council who was strongly in favour of encouraging women in business – this was still a relatively new phenomenon in the 'nineties.

On the grounds of my disability, permission was finally granted with the proviso that the premises could only be used for business purposes for the time I was in control. I also applied for the bizarre house name 'Ranmill' to be changed to 'Heron House'.

Conversion

I had reserved some capital from the sale of the bungalow for the garage conversion. A kitchen was installed in the rear third of one half of the double garage so that staff could make themselves drinks and heat food without going into the house. The up-and-over doors were removed and a barge board frontage with windows and a door were installed in their place. A lining for insulation, and a ceiling giving loft space and further insulation, were also added. I had a set of mirror-fronted wardrobes superfluous to need in the new house as it had fitted wardrobes in all the bedrooms. I had planned to sell these but suddenly realised they would make ideal storage for stationary and the like. They provided the additional advantage, being set up against the rear wall of the office, of making the office space appear to be twice its actual size. Cork boards for notices and information were placed on the walls and carpet fitted. I bought a set of smart black wooden desks in the sale at Habitat and we had a very professional-looking office at last.

There was another advantage to this conversion: it would not take much to alter it to become a self-contained annex should I, or anyone else, wish to do so at some later date. It already had a kitchen, and a shower and toilet could easily be installed because the cloakroom, with easy access for plumbing, was situated on the opposite side of the wall where the garage, now office, adjoined the house.

A Little Gold Mine

All my fears regarding a poverty-ridden future were being gradually lifted from my shoulders in a way I could never possibly have envisioned. I had a business that seemed to be on the way to doing well – at least well enough to provide me with a living income, but competition was mounting. And by some strange quirk I found myself living in a four-bedroomed house. It was truly beyond belief.

Where this next thought came from I can only guess. My children were now at University and beyond. It was a great sadness to me that when I had at last achieved a proper home they were no longer around to make it theirs too, so…. I had bedrooms to spare! What better than to advertise for lodgers. Not only would they provide me with income to help towards the rather heavy mortgage debt, but they would provide an element of companionship and security.

House Guests

The room I use for lodgers has a double bed, sofa, chests of drawers, fitted wardrobes with plenty of storage, a TV, and the option of a desk or table if required. Nowadays, they have sole use of the family bathroom except for when I have visitors, and they had shared use of the kitchen and utility facilities. Most of the applicants that passed through the doors of my home were single young men, many of whom were on the move with their jobs. Quite a few arrived because of broken relationships and often I found myself being used as a sounding board for their woes (the listening ear again!). Some were business men who returned home at weekends.

Friends worried about me having strangers living under my roof, but my instincts in judging people, that had been honed even further with practice through my work, proved invaluable. I kept the pendant for the personal alarm over my bed as a precaution but it was very unlikely that someone dependent on me for the roof over their head would try anything on.

I made very few bad judgements except for one occasion when I allowed my heart to rule my head. This happened with a 17-year-old whose Mother hen-pecked him mercilessly at the interview. It turned out that he had been living with grandparents because his Mother had remarried and had started a new family. The new husband didn't want him living with them. When he turned 16, the grandparents shed their responsibility and emigrated to France, apparently considering they had done their duty by him. He had just started a good job at County Hall, having moved from Cromer, but I insisted on a guarantor because of his age, and the new husband somewhat reluctantly stumped up. He seemed determined not to have the boy living with them - I was soon to find out why and eventually had to ask him to leave!

The RSPB

For many years, I had an unacknowledged contract with the RSPB Strumpshaw Reserve located three miles down the road. The first employee came into the office for Heron's services as he was looking for a single bedroomed flat in the area. These are rare outside of the city and I told him I could offer him lodgings as a temporary measure until he found something more suitable to his needs. He remained for the duration of his employment at the Reserve (as did many other lodgers who applied under similar circumstances) and he subsequently passed on my name to the person taking his place. These lads worked for either six or twelve month stints before moving on to a different reserve, and for many years each passed on my name to the next.

Sadly, this string of regular RSPB house guests (for they are not tenants when the property owner lives under the same roof) came to an end when the Buckenham Rail Station closed. The RSPB not only manages the Reserve but also the marshes beyond where the Station is located, just a short distance away from the Reserve headquarters. The old Station Master's cottage became redundant and was bought by the RSPB for use as accommodation for their staff.

The RSPB lads were great to have around – very quiet, tidy and respectful. Birds were their life and their love. One guy in his 30s had two Degrees, one being from Cambridge University. His salary was a mere £11,000 per annum but he fancied no other job. Even on their days off, and despite the young age of some, they spent their time 'bird watching' – never, seemingly, other than the feathered variety.

An Arranged Marriage?

I was not so fond of having women as lodgers – they tended to take over the house and particularly dominated the kitchen. This included a highly qualified Indian civil engineer, Ramyata, or Ramya as she preferred to be known, who came some years later. She arrived for the interview accompanied by her boyfriend, Naga, also Indian. He was continuing his studies at Dundee University where they had met. She not only spent a lot of time in the kitchen, but wanted her possessions to spill out from her room as she maintained she had insufficient space. No one before had ever complained to this effect. Also, because she claimed that her work allowed her no time to go to the gym, she would regularly pace the landing in the evening, and often there were thumps and bumps as she did who knows what sort of exercises up there.

Eventually I found myself again in a counselling role when she wanted to become engaged to Naga. Nightly she would shed tears because her parents had an arranged marriage in line for her back in India and they would not give their permission for her to marry Naga - he came from a lower caste. The problem was eventually resolved through the mediation of an aunt with whom she was close, and who obviously had persuasive powers.

My patience with Ramya was eventually rewarded when she insisted I should attend her wedding in her home town of Nizamabad, well off the tourist trail, in Southern India. It was south of Hyderabad (also known as 'Cyberbad' by geeks across the world as it is the technology centre of India). We stayed in Hyderabad for a couple of days on arrival, to enable us to get over the jetlag. Although Nizamabad is only some 60 miles away from Hyderabad, because of their terrible roads it took three hours by taxi, the principle means at the time of getting from A to B for tourists in the area.

Indian hospitality

The wedding was an experience my accompanying friend and I shall never forget. The night before the wedding we were invited to the bride's parents' house in the evening to join the family celebrations and, following Ramya, we had our arms traditionally decorated with henna. The following day, from 11am (Ramya had been there hours earlier and was previously at the Temple at something like five in the morning), we joined her as her guests of honour at this pageant of a wedding.

We had to sit with the bride-to-be all day as she welcomed her guests – of which there were in total 4,500. Half the town seemed never to have seen a white person before, and we were pawed and ogled at like a pair of strange exhibits, even by some of the politicians. But it was an extremely exciting and colourful experience. Interestingly, it was her Uncle and Aunt who hosted the event, her parents taking a back seat. The hotel they had booked us into, the only one in the town, was another experience!

Cell Block H

On our arrival at the hotel we were handed a large key at Reception and had to mount a wide set of stairs as there were no lifts. On reaching the landing, we discovered that each room had four-inch padlocks hanging from their doors. The landing was long and dark with a window only at each end, giving it the semblance of a prison cell block.

We unlocked our door with the huge key to find, on the inside, an eighteen-inch bolt for locking from the inside. The beds were low pallets with a thin 2" mattress, and the window was 80% blocked by the air conditioning unit. We found this so noisy at night that we had to decide whether to be kept awake by the excessive heat if we turned it off, or the unbearable noise if we left it on.

There was, however, an en-suite with shower, basin and toilet. After six times of asking at Reception for toilet paper, it appeared they had none, and we ended up, as the Indians do, washing down with the bucket provided after using this latter facility. This was the only hotel in town and Ramya's family had booked us the top-quality room – one with air-conditioning! We renamed our sleeping quarters 'Cell Block H' which was not far off the mark at all.

~

REFLECTION:

CONVERSION, RISK & TRUST

Conversion is the outcome of dramatic change. It has its risks and its rewards. Sometimes we need to make these changes ourselves which can be hard - it is taking a step into the unknown.

I had never had the experience of making decisions regarding large sums of money. I could have turned down the insurance guy's mortgage offer as being too financially risky. Conversion of my thinking had led me, instead, to trust the confidence he had in my potential to afford the mortgage he was offering. Conversion of my garage into an office led to a greatly improved business situation. The risk was that, if the business did not continue to do well, and I could no longer afford the mortgage, I could lose my home - at best I would have to downsize. The only way I could give myself a chance was to try. I worked on the theory that if things did go pear-shaped financially, I would still have had the advantage of knowing I had at least tried, I would have gained in experience and, overall, I would be in a better personal situation than I had been before.

At other times, unforeseen events out of our control can lead to a conversion. With the spiritual conversion that happened in my 'teens I had to do nothing. It just happened – it was God-led. It may not have happened without the dramatic change of my lifestyle from energetic teenager to bed-ridden invalid, but that was outside of my control too.

St Paul had one of the most dramatic conversions in the New Testament. Known as Saul, he had spent much time persecuting the Lord's disciples, issuing murderous threats against them. The Lord had other ideas for him. In a dramatic experience on the road from Tarsus he was struck by a bright light, he fell to the ground and heard the Lord speak to him. The first change he encountered was that he could not see, nor did he eat or drink for three days until the Lord instructed Ananias to lay hands on him. Immediately his sight and health were restored, and he was baptised. Bearing in mind his past, to follow the Lord was a big step to take – he was much feared initially by the disciples, he had to abandon his previous friends and influential contacts, and he was to suffer much in the Lord's name - he could have refused the Lord's request. Instead he became one of the most prolific and best known Christian preachers of all time. (Acts 9:1-22)

THOUGHTS FOR DISCUSSION

1. Think about any conversion you may have undergone. Do you believe it was God-prompted?

2. Did it involve much of a challenge?

3. If there is a challenge that you have turned down, or a prompting you have ignored, how has that made you feel?

--ooOoo--

Chapter 11

IMPROVEMENTS

NOT THE NHS

Susan Revisited

I had been seeing my remedial masseuse, mostly on a weekly basis, for a handful of years and by the late 'nineties very minor mobility advances began to manifest. Susan is a very caring and skilful practitioner, and from her initially I learnt a huge amount about my condition, and, more importantly, how to manage it.

Despite my deep desire to know what Susan thought the future held for me, she would never tell me anything negative, but she never tells an untruth – she would simply turn the conversation to something positive. It is probably very difficult to know exactly what direction the condition could take.

Susan eventually tried to persuade me to get in touch with an Iridologist/nutritionist she knew whom she thought would be additionally helpful to me. Being ever sceptical, and not able to afford to pay out more money, it took me some eighteen months before deciding anything was worth a try to better my situation. Affordability is very subjective – I began to realise that, even if I spent 25% of my total income on healthcare, it was better than having no income at all - which was the alternative if I did not keep myself fit enough to keep working.

Margaret

An Iridologist studies the irises in one's eyes and can tell from them what is going on internally in the body. From her findings, Margaret devised a diet for me that she said would help my condition and suggested I began with a month of detoxing – no alcohol or coffee at all!

I survived the month and very gradually eased into the diet. Still being somewhat sceptical, it took me at least another year before I began to follow the diet quite rigidly. Eventually I was to make a discovery that proved she was talking sense. For years I had suffered badly from acid indigestion and often reflux. Gaviscon was a regular bedtime intake as some people imbibe their warm cocoa. I discovered that when I followed the diet in the way prescribed, I had no need of the nightly antacids. Whenever I defaulted on the diet, back would come the indigestion and reflux. I had never been over-fond of milk, disliking tea unless it was served neat, and milk and milk products, it seemed, were amongst the greatest of the offenders.

Chocolate, sweets and wine were also on the 'no-no' list, as were all vegetables from the Solanum family; potatoes, aubergines, tomatoes, peppers, etc. Acid fruits such as oranges, grapefruit, mandarins and most of the berries were also to be avoided. Wheat products were to be watched and, if consumed, should be taken in their whole-wheat form. Brown rice, unrefined sugar, and whole wheat pasta, were among the recommendations, as was to eat as close to nature as possible, i.e. avoid processed foods or anything with additives. It was quite a tough call but eventually I did begin to note a difference.

Complementary Medication

Margaret also gradually weaned me off the National Health prescribed medication (my GP was duly informed and agreed, if somewhat sceptically) replacing each tablet with its more natural equivalent. The first of these tablets to be abandoned was a night-time pill the Doctor had told me was an additional painkiller that would help me sleep. Margaret told me that it was mainly an anti-depressant – I had not been depressed for some years by this time, so this was the first to be replaced. After a few days, my energy levels began to increase dramatically. The doctor's prescribed medication was keeping me suppressed, besides whatever else it should have been achieving!

Previously, on days when I did not have to struggle to be up for work, I could happily stay in bed, dozing until at least the middle of the day. On my new pill regime, I had greatly increased energy levels, and with more energy I could cope with more pain, therefore I became a bit more adventurous in attempting to increase my mobility.

Progress was very slow but, combined with the deep tissue massage, advances were made none-the-less. After another eighteen months or so, Margaret suggested an expensive supplement that she thought would additionally help me. It was supposed to revitalise the cartilage. I was already paying quite an amount for the alternative supplements, as well as the cost for the remedial massage on a fortnightly, and sometimes even weekly basis if the need arose. I was therefore somewhat reluctant to increase my expenditure yet again.

I eventually succumbed to Margaret's recommendation as, although a little improved, the pain I was experiencing was still beyond reasonable tolerance limits – and this despite being told many times that I have a high pain threshold. I was told this new formula would take two to three months to take effect. After two and a half months I was convinced I noticed slightly less pain in my neck, and very gradually my general physical condition continued its slow improvement.

My scepticism regarding the practice of iridology was further put to rest when, some years later, something Margaret had told me came to fruition. She said she had picked up what could be a slight gynaecological problem that was not serious but she felt it would do no harm to have it checked out. I didn't. About six years later, I did begin to experience some symptoms which were kept under observation by the hospital, and the cause was eventually treated by some minor surgery.

Water therapy

I had continued with my swimming regime throughout, latterly accompanied by a friend in case of difficulty. By this time, I was attending the Leisure Club at one of the local hotels. The pool had a deep end which was great for giving my spine a good stretch which seemed to suit it. The Leisure Centre had a very glamourous ladies' changing room and a lovely sauna, steam room, and Jacuzzi. It was in this Jacuzzi that I encountered the man who was eventually to change my financial status dramatically.

Meanwhile, the hotel management decided, in the light of new EU rules, that instead of having a permanent life-guard on duty as was now required for such a pool, they preferred the alternative of standardising the pool depth to meet the new regulations. Unfortunately, whoever was responsible had caused the level to be shallower than the required 4.2 metres depth. This had the unpleasant result, for the likes of those with spines lacking full flexibility such as mine, of causing one's feet to scrape the bottom whilst attempting to swim.

The Amsterdam Brothel

With their refurbishments, they also spoilt all the other facilities that had made it such a pleasurable place to relax during an evening after work. The sauna, in particular, which had previously been in a separate area at basement level, was replaced by an oversized box-like structure which was placed on the raised poolside restaurant area, thereby reducing the overall restaurant space. At the same time, the human element was completely withdrawn from this leisurely eatery. Leisure users previously could eat restaurant-style meals there without changing from their swimwear, so long as they were wrapped in the towelling gowns provided as part of the membership. Now this reduced eating area was replaced by robotic machines that dispensed drinks and sandwiches.

The humorous side of the replaced sauna, now fully visible to all using the pool and poolside areas, was that it had a large window and, inside, fancy flashing coloured lighting had been installed. The lounging shelves were at window-height which had the unfortunate effect, when the shelves were occupied by scantily clad bodies, of making the whole contraption resemble an Amsterdam brothel! Members were less than happy with the refurbishments and many, including myself, voted with their feet.

Aquafit

After exploring a few options, my next venue was Greens on Barrack Street in Norwich. By this time (2004), my improvement, aided by two Fischer sticks, offered sufficient security to negate the support previously provided by an escort. The ambience there was much more person-centred, perhaps because the sole focus was on fitness, whereas the hotel's principal focus at that time was their overnight guests, their restaurants, and their golf facility in that order, with the leisure area being their lowest priority.

Members of staff at Greens were very friendly and helpful. During one of my visits, one of the poolside attendants, noting my sticks, came across to chat with me. He had something of a back problem himself. During the conversation, he mentioned the Aquafit classes they ran three times per week and thought they might be helpful to me. I explained that I did not think I could manage three quarters of an hour without head support as my neck, though somewhat improved, was still very weak.

As all the classes were included in the monthly membership fee, the attendant suggested I had nothing to lose by giving them a try, reminding me I could always leave the class at any time if I found I could not cope.

I gave it a go. I found that when my neck started to ache, I would lean back and rest my head for a short while on the large pool divider. After many months of participating in these classes, at least two, if not three, times a week, I gradually found I needed this support for my neck less and less. The buoyancy of the water was a great enabler, the exercises a great strengthener, and, no doubt, the expensive supplement I was taking daily was continuing its good work. Many have been the times when I have attempted to do these pool exercises on dry land, without success.

FOOT LOOSE

Masai Barefoot Technology

There was one further aid I cannot ignore that contributed to my overall improved wellbeing and mobility. This was the discovery of MBTs. These are specially designed shoes using Masai Barefoot Technology (MBT). I had offered to do a good deed for a neighbour who had been one of my regular walking escorts. It had been rather unsafe for me to venture out on walks on my own in case of falls. Maggie had been a great walker and bird watcher in her time, and frequently took me – or rather I took her as she didn't drive - for short

214

walks, sometimes locally (no car needed) or further afield to more interesting areas of the Norfolk country or seaside.

Maggie had seen an advertisement for these special MBT shoes and she wanted to try some for her walking holidays. When she mentioned the price they were sold at – in excess of £100 – I knew they were not for me. £60 for the comfort of Ecco sandals was already the peak of extravagance in my book.

These MBT shoes were not sold through retail outlets and the only place they were available to be seen locally was down in Beccles, Suffolk, where there was a trained dealer operating from a church hall. Maggie had done me many good turns so I offered to drive her down to Suffolk.

The Clumpy Dumpy Shoes

We arrived at the hall to find various people in clumpy-soled shoes, extolling the virtues of this rather hideous-looking footwear. Maggie tried some on. Various instructions were being given to those testing the footwear as to how to walk correctly in them, and all this took some time. To kill the waiting, I decided I had nothing to lose by having a go myself.

I could not believe the difference these shoes made to my feeling of wellbeing and improved ability to walk. I was dependent on two Fischer sticks at the time, and I felt I could have almost discarded them both there and then. The shoes are designed to mimic the Masai's way of walking – in their native land they continue to walk barefoot in soft sand or earth as humans were originally designed to do. This negates the stresses to joints caused by walking on hard surfaces in flat soled shoes as is the modern way. The MBT shoes had thick curved soles with what they referred to as a 'pivot point' in the middle, and heel sensors at the back that absorbed beautifully any impact from contact of the heel with the ground.

I was soon to learn that it is through the heel that most of the back pain seems to emanate. With most flat-soled shoes the whole of one's foot is approximately 75-80% in constant contact with the ground when walking, and 100% when standing. Because of the curved sole of the MBT, each part of the sole is approximately only 30% in contact with the ground at any one time – even when standing. It did not take me long to realise (despite my reverse logic!) that this equalled over 50% saving of pressure on my spine. By the same calculations, they also helped the soles of my feet as I had quite severe metatarsalgia since my mid-30s and my feet were painful to walk on too. Metatarsalgia is where the lining has all but disappeared between the metatarsals in the foot and inflammation sets in.

I bought a pair of these shoes there and then at a cost of £125. It was the month of May. The shoes looked like some issue from a hospital podiatry clinic: black, with a deep toe box and lace-ups – quite ugly. I soon gained the confidence to walk round the block on my own, but as summer got underway I found myself creeping out in the evenings, in the dark, to take my daily exercise, because the heavy black shoes looked very silly with summer outfits.

The Shoe Seller

In retrospect, I wondered just how much my bad feet had exacerbated my spinal condition because of walking awkwardly. Within two months I had bought a second pair – sandals this time, and my thoughts went into business-mode once again. There must be hundreds of people with all sorts of musculoskeletal problems who would benefit from these shoes. There was only one dealer in Norfolk and she operated from her Pilates Clinic in Holt, North Norfolk.

I went to a taster training day in London for would-be trainer-dealers, and decided I would like to be able to help others by selling these shoes back home. The staff at Head Office were rather sceptical, bearing in mind my condition, and suggested I should do it in partnership with someone. I was still operating my lettings business so knew I could call on any help from the staff there if needed.

To begin with, I saw my 'shoe' clients in my lounge and sold them alongside the management of my lettings business. This time, I was not the first in Norfolk setting up a new style of business – I was the second, and pretty much creamed the local market initially yet again. And again, as many of these clients came with chronic conditions of varying sorts, I became a sounding board for their woes, and a source of suggestions for gaining further help.

MOVING FORWARD

Upgrading

My car needed replacing and I bought, for the first time, a brand-new car which I expected to run into the ground, hopefully some twelve or so years hence. It was a Citroen Picasso which, size-wise, seemed an extravagance when mostly for use by one person, but I needed the space for loading the wheelchair into the hatchback area. I also needed the comfort afforded by these larger models: the arm rest, good suspension, ease of getting in and out, etc. I looked on this extravagance as a call to offer lifts wherever I could. This offer was invariably taken up when car-sharing was being arranged among friends because their cars could not accommodate my chair, so I had little option but to drive anyway.

When I first looked at a Picasso there was no automatic version. I was told Citroen was in the process of developing one. Changing gear and using a clutch, although manageable for short distances, was not conducive to the well-being of my spine, so I ordered one and had to wait three months before this first Picasso automatic came off the production line. It was an '03 registration. For an estate-type car, or people carrier as these were more commonly known, it had a very smart appearance, and was almost dateless in style.

A further few months on from taking possession of the car, its need in terms of wheelchair transporting, to some extent, became redundant. With the improvements that were beginning to manifest in my spine, I began to think of abandoning the use of the wheelchair and revert once again to a high-backed, lightweight, folding garden chair. This was less cumbersome and not so difficult to manage, and somehow seemed to be a less daunting prospect for those whom I visited for an evening of Bridge or other social occasion. In particular, the garden chair would be less of a problem for those who were fussy about their carpets! It also meant I didn't have to drive every time there was a car-sharing event.

Using a garden chair instead of a wheelchair did present a problem for the holidays I was beginning to take. A wheelchair is an acceptable disability aid and not charged for, particularly when flying. A garden chair, however, was classed, and charged for, as an additional item such as when taking bikes, skis, etc. to foreign climes. Another disadvantage is that a garden chair folded for carrying is less easy to unfold and sit in for short temporary periods. Although my ability to stand had increased from a few seconds to a few minutes - thanks to the MBT shoes which were now my standard footwear - it was still not sufficient to cope with queues at airports and the like.

Improvements

Thanks in no small part to the ministrations of my remedial masseuse's gifted fingers, the Iridologist/nutritionist's wise advice and supplement suggestions, my exercise regime, a comfortable car to drive about in, and general assistance from those around me including the aids provided by PACT – all of which minimised stress

- my muscle tone continued to improve. The special formula suggested by Margaret - Collagen Plus, which is a strong formula of collagen, chondroitin and glucosamine, costing around £1.00 per day, and which was purported to 'revitalise' the joint cartilage – in my case chiefly the discs between the vertebrae - was obviously working too. The constant, extreme pain I had been suffering, particularly in more recent years, gradually eased, and what remained became more a discomfort – so long as I kept within the bounds of 'sensible' activity and avoidance of stress to my body. I found myself more and more able to do things I had not been able to do for years.

The National Health Service

My only complaint is why the NHS Consultants had not advised that some improvement could possibly be achieved if one could afford to pay for treatment rather than leave one with the miserable, hopeless, diagnosis that had been meted out to me. But then the remedial masseuse I attend is exceptionally gifted. She clears the build-up of calcium in the muscles caused by stress from overuse (in my case this doesn't take much – overuse, it seems, is because the muscles have to over-compensate for the weak skeletal structure). She is able, by careful manipulation, to readjust any vertebrae that shift out of alignment and clears any spurs that may be developing. She has been able to treat some of the frightening situations my neck gets into, despite the hospital advising that it is too dangerous to allow anyone to touch it. But then Susan is highly qualified as well as gifted, and I trust her talents implicitly.

Without Susan's regular ministrations I wonder what state my body would be in today. Quite possibly it would be as the National Health Service implied all those years earlier. Does this imply that National Health staff are insufficiently trained to manage such conditions? Or maybe it is the long-term cost implication.

A TRAVEL TALE

Travel Prospects

As things continued to improve, I began to think of life beyond my business. Over time I had received invitations from several of my overseas landlords to visit them in the varied countries in which they lived, but knew my condition made it impossible. Besides, I was a great believer in not mixing business with pleasure.

Then one year, a landlord based in Penang, Malaysia, rang me up on several occasions around Christmas and New Year, always beginning her conversation about the weather. "What is it like with you? It is 31C here" knowing full well we were enduring icy conditions. "Why don't you come out? I can arrange some good accommodation at a discount." Her husband held a senior administrative position in the RAF based in Penang, the island just off the mainland of Malaysia. In retrospect, I gathered she was quite bored as an expat out there.

After the third phone call along the same vein in almost as many weeks, and the ground outside covered with snow and ice, I began to think, why not? I had always wanted to travel and I began to think that with, by then, a quite noticeable improvement in my spine, I could probably manage a flight of that distance, especially as it would be quite a relaxed holiday once there.

Succumbed

I, and the friend who accompanied me, were royally treated for the duration of our stay. Accommodation had been booked for us in the Eastern & Orient Hotel, sister to the famous Raffles Hotel in Singapore. We were paying a pittance for B & B accommodation in a suite overlooking the Bay. Not only did we have a bedroom with queen-size twin beds, but a good-sized lounge area too – and a massive bathroom to die for. It had a huge Jacuzzi-style bath, 'His

220

and Hers' washbasins and large 'His and Hers' walk-in showers (in our case it was Hers and Hers), and much to my friend's intrigue, a phone in the bathroom – and another in the loo! At the special rate my landlord had arranged for us, we were paying no more than for a very average B & B in the UK.

We were taken out on alternate days by my landlord, and made our own arrangements on days in between. We had a truly good time visiting various places, including the mainland. We were invited to lunch at the Penang Club, and we were also introduced to the more native-style of eating where food was placed on banana leaves, and even directly on the tables and eaten with fingers. We did and saw far more than we would have done had we been left to our own devices, thanks to the kind hospitality of our hostess.

Repercussions

Eighteen months down the line, my business was to battle with the repercussions of accepting this hospitality. The property we managed for this landlord and her husband was quite a large one, and commanded an equivalently high rent and deposit. We had some very good tenants in the property who had looked after it meticulously. The owners, our hosts in Penang, were returning to the UK permanently and wished to repossess their home so that they could move back in. This was no problem for the tenants who were moving into a house they were buying that happened to be in the same road.

However, there materialised one problem for us as a business. On her return, our landlord was attempting to find every reason to acquire the tenants' deposit. By rights, and in my view, having done the check-out inspection myself, it should be returned to the tenants in full. This was before the Tenancy Deposit scheme in operation today that guards against such unscrupulous landlords.

I could not do other than make a fair judgement, and I knew the landlord was trying it on as some sort of repayment for the hospitality she had granted me and my friend during our stay in Penang. Except that it was not me she would be penalising – it was the tenants who would be the losers. When I told her my decision, she verified my assumption and accused me of being ungrateful for all she had done for us. She became quite unpleasant and threatened to take the matter further. Hating conflict – and she lived locally – I rather wished I had stuck to my original principle of not mixing business with pleasure!

The matter was to be resolved in an unexpected way.

$$\sim$$

REFLECTION:

WATER & HEALING

"… and the Spirit of God was hovering over the waters." (Genesis 1:2)

There is something very wonderful about water - it is such an essential part of God's bounty for us that His Spirit hovered over the oceans at the Creation. When we are born, we emerge from water, the amniotic fluid from our Mother's womb. More than 50% of our bodies contain water (it varies at different stages of life); it is necessary for us to drink plenty of water to remain hydrated and in good health, and water is the most natural cleansing agent. Salt water has great healing properties for wounds and skin ailments. There is a belief that some of the trace elements in certain waters have deeper healing properties and many have attended spas and baths dedicated to such treatments.

No wonder, then, that Jesus uses the image of water so frequently in His teaching. Ever mindful of His followers' physical needs and enjoyment, He turned water into wine at the marriage feast in Cana (John 2:1-11) – the first of His recorded miracles. He Himself was baptised in the waters of the Jordan (Matt 3:13-17). He walked on water, and tested Peter's faith by suggesting he did likewise (Matt 14:22-32). Positioning Himself at Jacob's well, He told the Samaritan woman He met there that whoever drinks the water He gives them will never thirst: "Indeed, the water I give them will become in them a spring of water welling up to eternal life." (John 4:13-14).

For me, water has become essential to remaining mobile. There are exercises that can be done in water that cannot be done on dry land. Being by the sea, with its constant gentle lapping waves, its mystery of depth and distance, is a great means of relaxation for the mind. It was the source of that great feeling of well-being and triumph after my New Year's Day paddle. Rivers, likewise, hold the secrets of where they have come from and the oft hidden agenda of where they are flowing to. And both teem with living creatures for our nourishment and enjoyment.

THOUGHTS FOR DISCUSSION

1. What does water mean to you?

2. Have you considered how essential water is to our lives, both physically, mentally and spiritually?

3. What other natural gifts of God's creation do you benefit from?

--ooOoo--

Chapter 12

FINALE

TOWARD THE END

The Pension

Thoughts about a pension to see me out to the end of my days had entered my thinking around the mid 'nineties as my profitability began to increase. I never earned a fortune from the business. It was enough to pay the mortgage and live a reasonably comfortable life – at least compared to what I had previously experienced whilst bringing up the family. A pension seemed the next logical step to start funding once I got to the stage where there was 'a bit to spare'.

I had a chat with my youngest brother who was employed as a Pensions Adviser at a small branch of Norwich Union (now Aviva) in Nottingham. "I wouldn't bother if I were you" he advised. "Bearing in mind your age, and starting to save so late in life, you might just as well rely on the Government". I told him in no uncertain terms that I would do all in my power to avoid having to rely on the Government again for an income. I'd had enough of that form-filling and intrusiveness in the past.

The maximum amount I could afford, I began to put monthly towards a personal pension. It was never going to provide me with a fortune but it would supplement to a small extent the State Pension one would get automatically at aged 60, the pensionable age for women at the time (one of the few advantages women had over men who had to wait until aged 65). However, sometime later the benefits of paying into a personal pension were reformed by the Government, and these reforms were not to my advantage. The Government had worked on the assumption that those nearer the beginning of their working lives would have plenty of time to make up the difference created by the changes, whereas those of my age would already have accumulated sufficiently sizable pots for the changes to have a negligible effect. Not so for me who started my pot so late (I was, by then, in my 50s).

I continued to pay in regardless. Hopefully, the eventual sale of my business might augment the total of my savings. I had no option but to trust that my financial future would be taken care of one way or another – just as it had been to date. I did not want to have to become a burden to my children or anyone else.

A Feather in my Cap

As society became more and more confident that the new Housing Act delivered all it promised, the lettings market grew and grew. New agencies were popping up almost weekly to cash in on the boom. Estate agents also jumped onto the bandwagon as they realised that when sales were down, another string to their bow was to be able to offer vendors the possibility of renting out their property until the market improved, thereby retaining control of the property and preventing the possibility that the vendors might move to another agency to attempt a sale.

The growing number of letting agencies had another consequence – competition became fiercer, therefore, and not far behind came the move towards take-overs. The 'big boys' wanted to become even bigger and began competing with each other for size. They started making approaches to the smaller fry. I was very small fry by comparison to most – a letting agent who did not own a single property of their own to rent out.

I had already been approached in previous years by some of the larger and better known estate agents and letting agencies with exploratory requests to buy me out - they had been turned away. I should have been flattered. Or maybe they had got to know of my poor physical condition and thought I would be easy meat - only too ready to offload what they must have considered to be a burden which I would welcome having taken off my hands for a sum. Little did they know! It was the business that kept me going, encouraging me to rise from my bed each morning. What else would help transfer my mind away from the pain and thoughts of the potential consequences of my condition?

The Lady is not for Selling

One guy, who was also a sole proprietor of a letting agency, was often in the Jacuzzi in the days of my visits to the Sprowston Manor Leisure Club. He would quiz me regularly about my health and how I was doing. He also liked to talk business. I used to think "You're a competitor - why should I engage in your questioning?" In retrospect, I think he was just being friendly. A few years later I bumped into him in Norwich and we had another amiable chat. He finished by saying that if ever I wanted to sell my business he would be very interested. "Yes" I thought, "you and many others".

I was not ready to sell. I had fought hard to create a means of income – I didn't want to see it disappear. I did NOT want to end up back on benefits, although this was unlikely to happen as, with a sale, I would have the resulting capital on which I would be expected to live, but it was unlikely to be sufficient to last me for the remainder of my lifetime, or to invest for a decent income. From what little knowledge I had gleaned regarding the valuation of my business, I assumed it most definitely would not.

Raison d'Etre

The business had become my 'raison d'etre' - apart from my family of course, but I could not be much help to them. When my grandson was born, the first-born of my many grandchildren to come, I had to be propped up in an armchair with my arms supported to be able to bear his little weight when I first held him. I remember feeling an instant rapport with him as he gazed into my eyes and gurgled his discontent about his uncomfortable first experience of a long journey in a car seat.

At the beginning of the new millennium, although my abilities were beginning to improve, I was not of an age to think of retirement. This physical improvement I was now experiencing was completely contrary to what I had been led to believe by the Health Service that had taken such a passive line with me all those years ago. As with the creation of the business, I trusted the good Lord had its termination, and my future, in His hands too.

Partnership

The approaches by these firms did trigger my thoughts about the future. Although I was not ready to relinquish control of my business altogether, that did not stop me from pondering how I could gradually wind down and eventually retire.

My mobility had begun to increase and the pain had lessened to some degree. The desire, and the ability to do things I had not been able to do for years, grew – going for days out, visiting museums and galleries, stately homes, the theatre. Even ordinary events such as high street shopping had been off limits without hiring a mobility scooter from Shopmobility in the Castle Mall in Norwich. And, of course, there was my passion for travel. If I was to begin taking on new activities I would have to think of working fewer hours. I still had to consider pacing myself.

A partner seemed the ideal solution. When the time was ripe, the partner could then take over completely and buy me out. They would, of course, need to find alternative premises as I had planning permission to use my converted garage for business purposes only for as long as I was in charge.

My children all lived away and neither the type of business nor its profitability was of sufficient interest to them. They have all achieved good careers; Michelle had become a much sought-after qualified NNEB nanny and eventually added to her achievements - by demand, not training – as a special needs teacher; Lis has a Business Studies degree and had settled into organising the tenders for a large nationwide construction company, and Paul, despite Norwich School's recommendations that he should attempt entry only to a polytechnic college rather than a university (reverse psychology, maybe?), had achieved a PhD in Electronic Systems Engineering at York University. As Senior Engineer, he heads a team working for a company at the spearhead of electronic technology. Combined with their marital partners, all were living very comfortable lifestyles - far better than I expect Heron, at least in its present format, could achieve for them.

A partner was not easy to find, nor easy to fund. I thought, also, about moving to more conventional premises now that I was physically better able to cope. That way, and now an established business, we would no doubt generate greater footfall which, in turn, would lead to more properties, increased turnover, and thereby the ability to salary a second person at managerial level.

Older Man

A friend of a friend was suggested as a possible partner – he was early retired with plenty of time on his hands, and plenty of energy that he needed to utilise, but it turned out he had little else to offer. I took him on initially as an employee. He found it hard to follow the defined rules we had for operating that ensured everything ran with (relative) trouble-free efficiency. It was not the system we had established maybe, so much as the fact that the suggested 'modus operandi' emanated from a woman that he found difficult to cope with. It was still relatively early days for the acceptance of women in business, let alone a woman running a business. After quite a few aberrations on his part I had to let him go before he damaged my business big time.

Younger Man

Some time later a young man came into the office wanting me to look after a couple of properties he had bought with money given him on his 18th birthday by his grandparents. He sat in my office and he was keen to chat as we arranged the formalities. During the conversation, he mentioned he would love to do the type of job I was involved in. I told him that I was looking for someone to train up to eventually take over from me. He showed quite a keen interest.

This young man was at City College following a Business Studies course and still living at home with his parents very locally. He asked what qualifications he would need for a career in management and letting. I told him it was hard to define as no university degree particularly applied, but the University of Life was a good starting point. The second, and maybe the most important for someone who had ambitions for taking over a business, was good business sense – something, it seems, you are either born with, or not. It can be learnt to an extent, and his college course would form an excellent grounding in this respect.

The advice I gave him was that if he was intent on following this career route he should go away and seriously think about it and come back after his final exams when he would be ready for employment. He said he would have a chat with his parents.

TRIAL AND ERROR

Career End

I had had no clear idea of how many years it would be before my running of Heron would come to an end – it was in the lap of the gods – God's lap in my book. Of course, I had dreams, but I had long since learnt that not all dreams materialise in the way we wish. The unexpected always seems to happen. My immediate expectation was to carry on for a few more years at least, training up a successor so that I could gradually start working part-time. Eventually, and hopefully, the partner would take over completely and, with a further bit of luck, buy me out, and then move the business out from under my roof. This young man (he was 19 years of age) had raised my spirits – he seemed the perfect solution. I hoped that he would remain interested when his studies finished in fifteen months' time.

With my gradually increasing new-found energy and ability I was quite looking forward to having my home completely back to myself and to begin leading a near normal life again. My focus had been almost solely directed towards the business over the years. It was something positive and rewarding that my differently abled body allowed me to do, given the unique environment of the business premises. The staff undertook the elements that were more difficult for me. The idea of working part-time would mean I could begin to introduce a few more interests into my daily life. This young man seemed an answer to prayer. I was planning well ahead (I was by this time 58) and expected to be in the saddle for some five or so more years before, albeit hopefully, off-loading most of my responsibilities and taking more of a back seat.

Impatience

The young man with the two flats - I shall call him Adam - was back within the week. He wanted to take up my offer but not after completing his final exams – he wanted to start immediately. He wanted to give up his business course. I told him I was quite happy to wait and would keep the place open for him – after all, people hadn't exactly been hammering at my door to take up the position. The business course would be an ideal foundation for someone his age. In addition, there would be plenty of opportunities for further courses from associations connected to the lettings industry, and free training from the local Council, once he was in employment. Broadland Council was very supportive towards small businesses and we had already benefitted in no small part from various grants and courses to date. But no, Adam was adamant; he did not like what he was doing at College.

Somewhat dubiously I let him start. Initially he was to be on a part-salary, part-commission basis – the latter so that he would have the opportunity to grow the business in order for it to be able eventually to support him on full pay. Most of the industry associates I had contact with thought what I was doing was a brilliant idea. A malleable young man, a 'tabula rasa' to train into sound letting and business principles – good fortune was indeed on my side once again!

Embarrassing Encounters

Before too long the offers for further training came pouring in; from 'Letsure' our insurers (this training was essential for him to be able to sell the landlord and tenant insurances), and from the local Broadland Council Business Training department. The Council at the time was running a scheme, a form of apprenticeship, that would have benefited me financially and him educationally. We were apparently the ideal size of enterprise to be beneficiaries from what was on offer. But for some reason, Adam was not interested. "I'm not an exam sort of person" was his retort.

I reluctantly passed on his refusal to take part in the scheme to the Council training personnel. The conversation ended with the suggestion that maybe if they came out and explained to him directly the benefits to himself, and to me as a business - that there were no exams, just a system of observation and suggestions - then maybe he would change his mind.

The interview, carried out in my office, was an embarrassment to say the least. He adamantly refused to take part in the scheme. I was becoming very disillusioned. He did not want the responsibility of selling insurances either. Twelve months down the line he had not brought in a single new property. I asked him why not? He said he did not know where to start. Trawl though the Yellow Pages, arrange interviews with solicitors, estate agents with no lettings departments, talk to friends, and parents' friends - spread the word about what you are doing!

It seemed he was incapable of being proactive. Many properties had come to me from the casual chat with friends, or at a party, or other such function not necessarily associated with lettings. It was very much a networking industry, particularly important if one did not have high street premises. At this point I gave up with him as a partnership prospect.

THE END OF HERON

The Entrepreneur

Sitting chatting over coffee with a tenant at one of my property inspections, the subject of my young colleague came up. This tenant had not seen him for a while and wondered how he was doing. I explained that he wasn't – yes, he did his daily job for the few hours he worked, but in terms of partnership, of the future handing over of the business – that was not going to happen. It transpired that this lad was too comfortable living at home, with top-up income from his rented flats, and an evening/weekend job putting together and selling bikes for one of the large sport stores. He was neither hungry enough, committed enough, nor ambitious enough – or maybe he was ambitious, but expecting not to have to put in any donkey-work in order to become the executive he aspired to. He expected life to be handed to him on a plate, as no doubt it had been done for him so far in his life by his doting parents and grandparents.

The tenant I was enjoying a coffee break with was something of an entrepreneur himself (what he was doing in a rented property I didn't ask) and was looking for something new to get his teeth into. To my surprise, he offered to buy the business from me. I was a bit stunned as I was not altogether ready to give up. However, as he pointed out, there would need to be a period of training. I explained he would need new premises because of the planning restrictions, but he seemed to think that would not be a problem when the time came for me to hand over completely. I wondered how well this man would be able to continue running the business with the high ideals for which Heron was renowned. But then there would be the period of training - and how often would I receive a direct offer for its purchase? I suggested he put an offer in writing and we would take it from there.

Auction

I had no idea how to handle such a situation. As it involved finance I thought my Accountant may be able to point me in the right direction. I rang him up and he surprised me by saying that he would be happy to handle the negotiations for me himself – it is part of what they, as an accountancy practice, did. We would need to do a valuation, and why not contact all the people who had approached me over the years in their attempts to buy me out? Some of the big firms in Norwich had wanted to purchase my portfolio as word must have got around of the valuable reputation and type of properties I held. No doubt, also, knowing of my disability they perhaps thought I would jump at the opportunity of handing over responsibility. When my condition was at its worst, I must say these offers were, at times, quite tempting.

The valuation of such a business, I was to learn, was on average twice the annual turnover. By this time, I had not far short of ninety properties on my books, most of them bringing in above average rents. I was quite surprised that the possible outcome of a sale was a lot greater than I had anticipated.

My Accountant wrote to the companies that had approached me in the past. Five of them were quick to return a response but one offer was very low so they got left by the wayside. The offers were almost double what my tenant had offered but he fought on for a short while and then had to drop out too. We were left with three, known as the 'big boys' in Norwich letting circles. What ensued was effectively an auction.

The Offers

I had to consider not only the money that would be achieved from a sale but I had a responsibility to my landlords too. Which of these companies would best offer the service that matched what my landlords had become accustomed to under Heron's wing?

Two of the companies offered me part-time employment which suited me as I was not ready to give up working altogether just yet, though I did wonder how I would cope with my seating needs. I decided to hedge this problem until details were finalised. From their point of view, the job offer was partly to ease across the properties and landlords. Properties, not to mention their landlords, had their foibles, and at Heron we always tried to accommodate some deviations from the norm of our management contract if these were requested. By offering me employment, these companies were buying my knowledge and expertise in these areas after the buy-out, to make life easier for themselves - and hopefully for my landlords.

I agreed to go for interviews. The first was a large local chain that had not too long been established but had grown branches at quite a phenomenal rate. I would be taken on as an employee and given the full training that befell anyone joining the company.

The idea of proper training quite intrigued, but being treated as a mere employee was a bit of a double-edged sword. How would I cope with this after having been my own boss for so many years? How would I feel if I considered my properties were not getting the treatment or tenants that I had pledged to my landlords they were worthy of? How would I feel taking orders from others, particularly as many would be, almost by default, younger than me? But a regular income, and the burden of overall responsibility lifted from my shoulders, had a great appeal. I was tempted. This company's offer was also the highest so far.

MICHAEL

Sole Trader

The second company remaining in the running with a high offer was a sole trader as I had been myself for most of my business life. In more recent years I had gone 'limited' at the recommendation of my Accountant as he advised there were tax advantages. With the additional accounting work involved I remained sceptical as to whether the tax benefits outweighed the extra work required. Accounts were not my favourite area of activity, my 'numerate dyselxia' and associated problems with logic no doubt being responsible for this antipathy.

The owner of this sole trader company was Michael, the chap I used to see in the Jacuzzi at the Sprowston Manor Hotel leisure centre. He had a single office in a reasonably high footfall area of Norwich. He seemed determined to win the auction.

The prospects offered by Michael were slightly different to the other remaining contender. I had to contact his Office Manager to arrange an appointment. How would I get on with her in a small office? The interview was conducted over a lunch invitation from Mike. It turned out I would be offered part-time employment here too, and employment also for my young employee, Adam, who would be working full time with responsibility for the properties I would be bringing over. I felt that this smaller company with a more personal approach would be the best option for my landlords, particularly as they would effectively still be managed by the original staff, albeit under a different umbrella.

Michael raised his offer, became the highest bidder, and I was caught. The final amount I was to receive for the company I had developed from scratch, after this amazing 'auction', was more than double the original offer from my tenant – a sum I could never have dreamed of. It was enough to invest to create a decent retirement income. Michael was subsequently to tease me that I had become his 'most expensive woman' – I had apparently cost him more than the divorce from his wife.

Angry Young Man

The impending take-over was obviously going to affect my young colleague. He was being offered employment as part of the package and he would be very useful as he was handling the basic finances as well as general office duties, and some of the inspections.

When I broke the news to him he was not pleased in the least. "You told me I could buy the business!" he exclaimed indignantly. I didn't quite tell him he was nowhere near sufficiently polished to take on the running of a business. Instead, I told him that if he wanted to put in an offer he could do so. He blanched when I told him the offer he had to supersede. I also told him I would need to know that the business would be run properly and he would have to find new premises which would add to his costs.

He seemed to think he could run the business from his parent's home – from his bedroom? As a business, we had developed way past that stage. I told him I didn't think that would be good enough. Nevertheless, he said he wished to discuss the matter with his parents.

Even with help from his grandparents he could nowhere near match the offer in hand – thankfully.

Celebrations

The final contract documents between Michael and me were signed in the April of my 60th year, two months before my actual birthday. I vowed to save an amount from the proceeds of the sale to have a big party. There was so much to celebrate. I had succeeded in business against all odds. I had succeeded in providing an income for myself for some eighteen years. By investing the sale proceeds I could now provide for myself for the future. The funds from sale would create a sensible income to supplement the very meagre pension from the small fund I had managed to accumulate to date. Thereby, I could release my children from the possibility of having to support me financially in the future. My health had almost miraculously improved (though I was by no means completely cured) and I could now begin a modicum of normal living again. And I had a 60th birthday to celebrate, and many, many friends to thank for all the support and encouragement I had received over the years.

It seemed to be a habit of mine to celebrate my birthdays some months after their actual occurrence. For my 40th I was in the middle of my University exams; for my 50th I was in the process of converting the double garage at my new home and moving the business into it; and for my 60th I was in the process of easing myself and my properties under this new umbrella. My spinal condition, though improved, still needed careful management so I had to do things in a measured fashion.

The New Regime

How did the properties fit under this new umbrella? The first major obstacle to overcome was my young colleague who had been offered ongoing employment as part of the package. He continued to confound me. No, he didn't want to accept the offer of employment and come across to the new firm – he didn't like the idea of working in Norwich, he didn't like the idea of working in a larger office environment.

After much persuasion, Michael managed to entice him for just three weeks to integrate the properties and our system to run alongside his own. Presumably he hoped that Adam would discover he enjoyed the environment and would stay. But he didn't.

My fears of becoming an employee myself after so many years were unfounded. The young members of staff, including the office manager, affectionately nicknamed me 'Auntie Annie'. Michael ran a good office – he had a great work ethic and had an easy style with staff, and there was plenty of light-hearted banter with the consequence that it was fun to work there too. He was quite a philanderer and kept reminding me that I was the most expensive of his women and, to his chagrin, the only one he had never managed to entice into a relationship with him. He was always interested in our families and particularly our love lives (or lack of them).

Problem Solving

I left Michael to resolve the situation of the landlord, our Penang hostess, who was attempting to unfairly extract the deposit due to be returned to her tenants. (Mr Landlord never featured in any negotiations regarding the property). It was as much Michael's problem now. Whether it was the new face, the newly named company, Michael's adept way with people, or merely the fact he was male, he managed somehow to get her eating out of his hand and the whole of the deposit was duly conceded to the tenants.

Michael also made sure I had a comfortable office chair that well supported my spine, but it was an office chair nonetheless and did not quite offer the full head support that would have been of greater benefit. Part of my responsibility was to cover the viewings and inspections of the properties - his and mine, though technically they were no longer mine. This was to ensure I did not spend too long sitting in the office but spent approximately 50% of my working time out and about, returning to the office to write up the reports and generally help.

I was given the title 'Property Consultant'. It was wonderful to be still so involved yet without any of the responsibility of running the company, and in such a friendly, easy-going environment too.

TRAITOR

After Sale Shock

Some weeks into the new regime, I was out and about in rural Broadland inspecting some properties belonging to one of the farming estates I had brought over. I usually reported to the owner at the farm office before leaving. Any of the findings would, of course, be followed up in writing. As I was chatting with this farmer he pointed to a brochure on his desk and said: "Are you aware of this?" I picked up the brochure and to my amazement the whole document was an exact copy, word for word, of my landlord contract, including a spelling error I had not got around to correcting. The only difference was that the company name had been changed.

The young man who had been in my employment, and who had worked for Michael for three weeks, was attempting to poach the properties that had been in my portfolio, now sold to Michael. He had stolen copies of the files off my office computer, including the landlord database, and was attempting to set up in business on his own. I was eventually to discover that he was in league with a local conveyancing company that had a very dubious reputation. He was friendly with the owner's son and it soon became obvious they were using him as a front. No wonder his excuses for not wanting to accept Michael's offer of permanent employment!

Michael was not at all happy when I returned to the office and told him what I had discovered. For myself, I was mortified as well as angry. I felt embarrassed that Michael had paid out so much for this portfolio – possibly even over the odds in his eagerness to win the battle - and was now in danger of losing some of it to this unscrupulous young man who had so often boasted about his honesty and loyalty. I had thoughts that Michael would, as a consequence, have the additional costs of having to take legal proceedings to stop these activities, particularly as there was a clause in the contract of sale preventing such activity. But of course, it did not cover employees, and young Adam had signed no such contract himself as he had not been intent on staying.

All for Nought

Michael, however, was far more sanguine than I. Apparently, he saw no point in taking any form of legal action. He saw Adam for the ineffectual character that he was and therefore of little threat. Instead, he went to find Adam one evening at his place of part-time work at the sports store, and embarrassed him by meting out a good dressing down about the immorality of what he had done.

In retrospect, judging by Adam's past performance, Michael was right. There was very little to fear from his business acumen, or rather lack of it. He succeeded in persuading only one landlord and her bedsit to move across from us. His website never showed more than three or four properties, no doubt two of them being his personally-owned flats and the others quite possibly belonging to those running the conveyancing company. Secretly, though, I had to give him credit for the fact that, albeit nefarious, his act showed he did have some gumption after all, even though he might have been a pawn in the machinations of others.

FUTURE

Many blessings

Despite my contract with Michael being for two years, I continued as his employee for a further three and then provided the occasional holiday or sickness cover. Nowadays, life is so full with other activities I do not miss too much the travelling around, visiting properties, the contact with the public and the office banter. However, when travelling out and about through the Norfolk countryside with family or friends, and we pass villages that used to be on my patch, and houses that were once under my care, I do have to admit to a certain feeling of nostalgia and maybe even a little pride as I remember the wonderful job that kept me going through difficult times.

Despite the considerable healing of my spinal condition, which I believe to be largely improvement to my muscle strength, and the keeping of the vertebrae into relative alignment by Susan, the underlying condition remains.

My mobility has improved and the pain level has decreased which is a huge bonus for which I thank God. Thanks must go also to all those who have prayed for me over time (including the Pope John Paul II – now sainted!) and I thank God for having placed all these 'helps to healing' in my path, sometimes by extraordinary means. Occasionally I wonder whether complete healing has not been bestowed on me because, knowing the personality with which I have been endowed, I would be up, off, and away. The quieter, more measured lifestyle that I am obliged to follow gives me more time to keep my focus on Him.

A Miracle?

Very occasionally, if there is a significant shift in my condition I am sent back to my Consultant. On one such revisit, some years after my initial meeting with him at which occasion he had palmed me off with palliative care, he was totally amazed to see me walk into his consulting room. I mentioned all the various alternative means (complementary is what I believe the preferred term to be) by which I had achieved such improvement; namely the regular remedial massage, the complementary supplements, the MBT shoes, the Aquafit and regular walking, etc.

He is a man of few words. On one occasion, he had been trying to offer me some temporary pain relief which I had heard made you feel a lot worse initially, and I had refused it on the grounds that my pain level was at its uppermost limit and I could not cope with any more, particularly for only a short-term gain. As I was about to leave, he said to me "The patient usually knows best". It seems that both he and my GP think my improvement is not far short of miraculous.

Once these improvements began to become a reality I found the experience to be quite traumatic and would find myself at times succumbing to tears. It was traumatic in a good sense, the tears being of unbelief and sheer joy at the amazement of what was happening to me, compared to where I had been - and to what I had been told was to be the likely future.

Remaining Problems

I still have to acknowledge I have a dodgy spine and my new-found strength sometimes causes problems to arise. I am advised (by Susan) to keep doing everything in moderation. Moderation is often difficult to judge as quite often the repercussions occur at some time after the event. My spinal muscles can go into spasm and if this occurs in the upper spine it has been known to cause my blood pressure to plummet to very dangerous levels. The Hospital never seems able to come up with a definitive answer as to cause as, by the time I arrive at A & E, the spasms have eased. I have also had periods of time (one lasted 18 months) when my consciousness is marginally impaired.

These episodes, I believe, occur because of pressure on a vital artery either by the enspasmed muscles or a vertebra that has shifted slightly. The shifting of the vertebrae in the neck and stress to the neck muscles can also cause very debilitating head pains, and even slurring of speech if allowed to become too advanced. And I do get occasional periods of numbness up the front of my lower legs and left foot, but it is intermittent.

Physiotherapy

When visits to the Consultant occur after some new occurrence, and he can see no obvious treatment or need for further investigation, he will sometimes send me for a session of physiotherapy. The impression I am left with is that he does not know what else to suggest. Usually NHS physiotherapy is limited to six sessions.

On the most recent such occasion, the physio I was sent to told me she would not touch me as she could end up doing me more harm than good. She certainly did achieve more harm and certainly no good, but not in the way she had intended to imply. Besides telling me what I should and should not do to ease my condition – in which I had already been well schooled over many years by Susan – she reminded me of the 'Sword of Damocles' that continues to hang over me, namely that I could end up becoming completely paralysed. The appointment was a total waste of time, and rubbing my nose into what could become my future had negative results in the form of subsequent depression - as I reported to my Consultant on my next visit.

There are two positives of knowing what the future might hold in this respect; one is that it has given me chance to prepare for what life might be like should it happen, and how I would cope and keep myself occupied (the Dragon Naturally Speaking dictation system would come to good use after all!); the second is that I presume paralysis would mean one would no longer feel pain.

The Bottle – Half Full or Half empty?

I have experienced first-hand the physical symptoms of old age – well before my time. The problem is that genuine old-age now sits closely on the horizon and with it one can expect all the normal degenerative conditions that accompany it – on top of what I have already. I don't relish the thought of what lies ahead with a body that has had such a negative head start – even should my condition treat me as kindly as it has done during the past twelve years.

These thoughts, and trips to the Hospital with reminders of the possible directions my condition could still take such as was meted out by this recent physiotherapist, invariably return me to a state of negativeness. The bottle half empty. Nowadays, however, the depressions are brief. I can usually force myself out of the cloud after a handful of days, especially when I get back home and back into my routine of living what I consider to be a reasonably normal life, or maybe it is what has become 'normal' – for me. I persuade myself into thinking of all the things I can do now which, in earlier years, when the condition was at its worst, I would never have dreamt would ever be possible again - the half full bottle.

Life Today

The 'chair on wheels' more recently provided is a somewhat more conventional wheelchair to the earlier ones except that it has a head rest and I do not use the leg supports. I still use the pressure relief cushion but provide my own specially chosen cushions to support my neck as the NHS seem to be unable to offer anything suitable. The collar is used nowadays mostly for driving or other means of travelling, unless the neck is going through a particularly bad phase, but I can't wear it comfortably for long.

How I conduct my life has to be very measured, ensuring there is a balance of exercise (Aquafit, walking, and the occasional Pilates class when in a good state), sitting to rest when necessary (preferably in my conventional electrically-operated reclining armchair), and getting up frequently to move around (much to the annoyance of my pet cat). This way I can mostly avoid the muscle spasms and near-blackouts, and minimise the discomfort. Even with the current wheelchair, I cannot sit for long periods without becoming uncomfortable as it does not recline (which is how the weight is taken off the vertebrae), but it is adequate for approximately an hour or so after which I need to get up and indulge in some movement.

Social life isn't always easy and one sometimes gets overlooked because of the 'inconvenience' of the wheelchair. At social mealtimes, I cannot talk sensibly to people either side of me as any periods of turning to the right, and particularly to the left, causes incredible strain with frequently the aforementioned results. However, there are other activities I can get involved in nowadays, and I find I veer towards those that suit my condition best, rather than those that would have been my preference.

Christ within

Occasionally I still get irate with the deprivations that the condition affords. God often bears the brunt of these angry phases. I jokingly blame Him for getting the blueprint wrong when it came to the design of my earthly body – and I hope and pray that when it comes to the resurrection of the body He will bless me with a better model! But if I focus on the reality that even Christ found it hard to accept what lay ahead for Him during His agony in the Garden of Gethsemane, and finally at the Crucifixion, then I become somewhat appeased.

Having personally experienced the power of prayer, I try to turn my 'bottle half empty' times of pain and fear, and feeling 'left out', to good use by offering these as a prayer for a particular person or persons in need. Sometimes I even feel that it is a privilege to have to continue with these sufferings. God has granted me immense blessings and healings, but, I believe, not a complete cure because He knows my character. I believe He wants to keep me close, and to do His work. He knows that if I were fully healed I might be up and away, accomplishing all the selfish desires of my heart, and would have less time for Him. To feel so chosen can feel like a great honour.

At Last a Fixed Abode

Among my many blessings I now count a comfortable house that I can at last call home - and I also have the means whereby I don't have to worry about the mortgage; it has recently been fully paid - well before the original payments schedule was due to end. I have been settled at this address now for over twenty-one years - longer than at any other address, including my childhood home. Over two decades of my life have been spent helping others find decent accommodation in their time of need, with a business - the creation of which was nothing short of miraculous. I can truly say that during these mid years of my life I have had experiences and healings that have been beyond belief.

I have a wonderfully supportive fraternity in the secular Franciscans, similarly with our Prayer Group and Diocesan Service Team of which I have been a member for some years. There are many other friendship groups; my local friendships created all those years ago at the local Primary School gate with whom most of life's traumas have been shared, my Aquafit group more recently created, who are also a wonderfully caring and fun-loving bunch. Then I must not forget my lovely family and the seven delightful grandchildren, my siblings and the myriad nephews and nieces, including some 'greats', who, unfortunately, all live at a distance. In recent years, we have also enjoyed annual family reunions with the Belgian side of the family, thanks to my one remaining Aunt, my Mother's youngest sister, who is only eight years older than me. I try and attend these when I can.

Much as I would love to be closer to my family, I fear it would be very hard to recreate the support that I currently have here; the friends, my remedial masseuse who understands my body better than anyone, my spiritual family who know my soul with all its faults and failings, and the local NHS, despite my feelings towards its short-comings regarding my condition, still holds the ultimate answers and the records, when things go badly wrong. I would also find it quite hard to leave the lovely East Anglian countryside.

And at last I feel reconciled and 'at home' with the Church that I fell out with so many years ago. It holds the core of eternal Truth and Mercy. I had to learn the hard way that members of its hierarchy are only human like the rest of us, with faults and failings just the same, but God loves us all regardless as we strive together to reach our final fixed abode.

~

REFLECTION:

HOME

Home is a very special place – a place of security, of relaxation, of stability. At least for some. If you don't own your own home, life is less secure or relaxed. You are living at the mercy and generosity of someone else, even if you are paying for the privilege. If you are living as a lodger, or in a hostel with other people around, it may be even less calm and dependable. In any of these cases, one never knows when you might have to move on. There are some who do not even have the opportunities of tenancies or lodgings and sleep on the streets or in underpasses and doorways. Even mortgaged homes can harbour uncertainties if one's income alters and repayments cannot be met.

In countries hit by war or other atrocities, owning one's own home does not guarantee safety or security. Jesus Himself experienced many of these insecurities. Born in a stable miles from home, and before returning to Nazareth, His family had to flee to Egypt to escape the wicked machinations of Herod (Matt 2:13-15). After a later period of childhood security in Nazareth, He became an itinerant preacher, wandering from place to place, presumably relying on the goodwill of family, friends and followers for His places of rest (like a modern sofa-surfer?), and quite possibly even sleeping under the stars.

There can be certain advantages to being of no fixed abode: one has the opportunity of encountering many and varied people (some good, some bad!), and gaining a variety of experiences such as one would not necessarily gain in the secure confines of one's own four walls. Those of us living in such fixed abodes often feel the need to take holidays or other excursions to obtain such experiences. We are all involved in journeying, some in search of an abode, others returning to or from their home. Our spiritual home, Heaven, is where we all hope our journey will eventually take us.

THOUGHTS FOR DISCUSSION

1. Have you ever felt the lack of security of not knowing where you are going to lay your head for the night? Maybe the campsite was full when you arrived, or your hotel was overbooked?

2. If you were given the news that you were about to lose your home, how do you think you would cope?

3. How do you think refugees feel, fleeing their native country, often having to leave possessions and even loved ones behind?

--ooOoo--